# FAMINE IN ZIMBABWE
# 1890-1960

by

John Iliffe

With best wishes
John Iliffe

MAMBO PRESS

MAMBO PRESS
Gweru, P.O. Box 779
Harare, P.O. Box UA 320
Gokomere, P. Bag 9213, Masvingo

FAMINE IN ZIMBABWE, 1890-1960

First published 1990

ISBN 0 86922 459 x

Printed and published in Zimbabwe
by Mambo Press, Senga Road, Gweru
1990

# CONTENTS

# Preface

This book is based on only a brief period of research and an inadequate knowledge of Zimbabwe. I nevertheless publish it for three reasons. One is that its subject is indisputably important. The second is that I have had to abandon plans to undertake further research in Zimbabwe. The third is that I have had unusually generous help. I am especially indebted to the staff of the National Archives of Zimbabwe, a research centre so efficient and helpful that one can do three times as much work in a given time as in most of the world's archives. Among individuals, David Beach has not only given his time, his encouragement, and his unique knowledge of the early history of Zimbabwe, but he also suggested one of the book's main lines of argument. Ken Wilson made detailed comments on the manuscript from a close knowledge of agriculture and scarcity in southern Zimbabwe. Terence Ranger encouraged me at a critical moment. Andrew Shepherd showed me unpublished work. I am grateful to all these and also to the Mambo Press for publishing a book which is less securely based on research than most of their publications.

Readers will see that, except in the title, I have used colonial place-names when writing of the colonial period. These old names survive in quotations, which cannot be changed, and it would be confusing to use two names for the same place. All the old names are shown on the maps.

*John Iliffe*
*St John's College, Cambridge, England*
*November 1987*

# CHAPTER 1

## The Problem of Famine

The best way to explain the argument of this book is to explain how it came to be written. In 1986 I visited Zimbabwe for the first time in order to learn as much about its history as was possible in two months. I was especially interested in its population history, for this presents three problems to a historian. First, the population was surprisingly small when Europeans invaded. The first rough estimate in 1904 suggested 561 927 indigenous Africans. A later census thought this estimate should have been 700 000.[1] Even if this would still have been too low and the real figure in 1904 was nearer 1 000 000, that would still have been remarkably small when compared with the 8 100 000 people of all races living in Zimbabwe in 1984.[2] The second problem for the historian, then, is why population grew so rapidly during the colonial period. And the third is why it grew so early in the colonial period. During the first decade of the twentieth century many observers thought that the African population was increasing. During the second decade almost everyone thought so.[3] A later census suggested annual growth rates of 2,3 per cent between 1901 and 1911 and 2,4 per cent between 1911 and 1921.[4] Even if these rates were greatly exaggerated by starting from too low a base, the fact that population grew at all between 1900 and 1925 probably made Southern Rhodesia, as it then was, unique in East and Central Africa, for it is generally believed that population elsewhere in the region declined, or at least stagnated, during the early colonial period.[5]

While reading in the National Archives of Zimbabwe and pondering these questions, I came across a series of files on famine relief during the early colonial period. They were vivid and detailed and they immediately connected with the questions in my mind. They showed that many people had died in early colonial famines, especially following the great insurrection of 1896-7, but that famine mortality had declined rapidly during the early twentieth century and had ceased almost completely after 1922. This suggested a possible key to Zimbabwe's population history: famine (often accompanied by epidemic disease) could have held down the population before 1900; the ending of famine mortality could have permitted the rapid population growth of the twentieth century; and the fact that mortality was checked so early in the colonial period — earlier than in other African colonies I knew — could explain why Southern Rhodesia's population increased so soon after European invasion.

This explanation would also fit neatly with three other considerations. One was a belief in the central importance of famine in African history which most historians had learned from the disasters of 1968-85. The second was that the most convincing account of population history anywhere in pre-colonial Africa, Professor Joseph Miller's study of Angola, argued that famine and disease had indeed been the chief constraints on population growth in an environment similar to Zimbabwe's.[6] Third, Dr David Beach had suggested that recurrent drought and disaster — *shangwa* or *nzara,* in the Shona terms — were keys to understanding Zimbabwe's history.[7] It all seemed to fit together.

It was clear, too, that the material in the National Archives bore on a debate about the causes and control of famine which has concerned historians, social scientists, and development workers since the nineteenth century. The debate originated in India, which experienced several appalling famines during the second half of that century. Indian scholars, led by R.C. Dutt, argued that although these famines were caused by drought, drought caused famine only because it acted on a society impoverished by British policies.[8] Over-taxation, uncontrolled free trade, railway construction, and other innovations not only drained wealth out of India but also destroyed the indigenous techniques, such as household granaries, by which Indians had previously protected themselves against scarcity. These changes, so Indian scholars argued, bore especially heavily on the poor and landless, who could not afford to buy food at famine prices, so that it was possible for people to starve to death outside well-stocked grain stores, as happened in Bengal in 1943-4. Whereas in pre-colonial India men had starved when there was no food, in colonial India poor men starved when they had no money to buy food which was available. The nature of famine itself had changed.[9]

A similar analysis has recently been applied to the history of famine in Africa, especially in Dr Michael Watts's work on Hausaland in northern Nigeria, an area with many environmental similarities to Zimbabwe. Watts accepts that famines in this region were chiefly caused by drought and occurred at intervals before colonial rule, but he stresses that the Hausa people possessed many methods of preventing crop failure or surviving it. Their agricultural techniques sought to minimize risk. They stored food. They pursued supplementary non-agricultural occupations. They lived in large families and practised mutual aid. They formed clientage ties with powerful men and expected state assistance in times of need. In the colonial period, so Watts argues, these resources were eroded, especially by the commercialization of agriculture and by the demands of an alien state which gave only token aid during famine and impeded the emergence of a truly capitalist agriculture whose productivity might have prevented food scarcity. As a result, famine became more common (although perhaps less severe) in twentieth-century Hausaland. For the poor, indeed, it was almost a permanent condition, a 'drone of continual food shortage'.[10]

Yet this is only one perspective on the history of famine. Another is again best stated for India, especially by Dr Michelle McAlpin.[11] In her view, India's late nineteenth-century famines were no worse than those before colonial rule. The important point was that from the beginning of the twentieth century famine ceased to kill large numbers of people, except in the special circumstances of Bengal in 1943-4. Scarcity continued to recur, but mortality did not. Control of famine mortality was achieved, she argues, through many of the same means which Indian historians of the earlier period had blamed for causing famine — railway transport, wider trade, a mobile labour market — but also by a general increase in wealth, improved medical conditions, and especially more efficient government. One element in the growth of governmental competence was the compilation during the 1870s and 1880s of the Indian Famine Codes, which set out procedures to be followed by officials in order to prevent or relieve famine.[12] Similar advances had already ended famine mortality in England in the seventeenth century — England's last 'famine that killed' took place in 1623 — and in Western Europe (with rare exceptions) during the eighteenth century.[13] The same advances, chiefly under Communist rule, have ended China's appalling famine mortality in this century, although with one terrible interruption in 1959-61.[14] McAlpin's argument has been much criticized, especially on the grounds that the technological capacity to control famine mortality was valueless unless the political will to do so also existed.[15] That is true, but the technological capacity was nevertheless indispensable.

Reading the files in the National Archives, I believed that I was watching the abolition of famine mortality in Southern Rhodesia during the first quarter of the twentieth century. I already thought that famine mortality had been abolished at that time, or slightly earlier, in South Africa, whose last major 'famine that killed' took place during the 1890s, but that story has not yet been written.[16] I thought, too, that famine mortality was brought under control in many parts of tropical Africa after 1925, but the only detailed account of this, in Sudan, was not yet published.[17] The chance to tell the story for Southern Rhodesia was irresistible, especially because the colony's records are unusually detailed because it was governed unusually closely.

I therefore did two things. I incorporated my initial impression of the colonial period into a general book on the history of poverty in Africa,[18] and I decided to extend my research on Zimbabwe until it would support a short book on the history of famine and its control there. This book is the result. It consists of accounts of the nine most serious food shortages between 1890 and 1960, the aim being to show how scarcity and its relief changed over the period. The book is based on official reports in the National Archives, supplemented from contemporary newspapers, mission records, and secondary works. That is a limited range of sources and it is therefore a limited book. Its perspective is largely that of the colonial government. Important questions raised by more thoroughly-researched studies of famine cannot be answered from these sources.[19] Further research may refute many of my conclusions.

As I have gone deeper into the documentary evidence, moreover, I have realized that my initial impressions were often wrong. The following chapters set out a more complicated history of famine in Zimbabwe. Its chief elements are as follows.

First, the sparse evidence from pre-colonial Zimbabwe suggests that deaths directly due to famine were uncommon.[20] Drought and scarcity were common enough, and so are oral traditions of their horrors, but hard evidence of mortality is scarce and virtually confined to those famines which were caused or worsened by violence. Except in those cases, the peoples of pre-colonial Zimbabwe appear to have established their own controls over famine mortality. The important evidence here comes from missionaries who lived continuously in Matabeleland from 1859.

Secondly, the history of famine in colonial Southern Rhodesia divides into three phases. The first, to 1922, saw much hunger. The chief mortality, in 1896-7, was due to famine caused by violence. There followed four famines — in 1903, 1912, 1916, and 1922 — which were mainly 'traditional' in form, in that they were due to drought and were worst in those areas least affected by the European presence, although colonial disruption was an increasingly important element as time passed. All these famines threatened severe mortality. None in fact caused it, partly because indigenous survival techniques persisted, partly because the colonial government gradually developed a system of relief comparable to (but apparently not drawn directly from) the Indian Famine Codes. Thanks to more efficient administration, transport, and trade, the famine of 1922 was the last in which any significant number of people died directly from hunger.

Yet the pattern of famine and relief established by 1922 almost immediately gave way to a second phase. This was a result of the triumph of European settlement. Signs of the change were apparent before 1922, but thereafter they were dominant. From 1930, at least, land alienation and population growth were reducing total African grain production per

10

head, although the effects were felt at different times in different regions. They appeared first and most severely in the area most disrupted by European settlement, Matabeleland, which now became the chief area of scarcity, along with remote pockets surviving in other regions. During the 1930s and 1940s, moreover, scarcity came to be concentrated especially among the poor and weak, taking the form not of famine mortality but of endemic malnutrition. Meanwhile the dominant settler economy also took over the relief of scarcity. In the famine years of 1933, 1942, and 1947, it was not the Native Affairs Department that dominated famine relief but the Maize Control Board, along with the White farmers who supplied the grain and the White traders who distributed it. Here lay the contrast between Southern Rhodesia and the Northern Nigeria described by Watts, for in Southern Rhodesia capitalism — *White* capitalism — did triumph during the 1930s and create a new, capitalist system of famine control to replace the indigenous system.

Yet in the 1950s the pattern changed once more and a third phase began. Scarcity remained similar in character but became more acute as the agrarian crisis in the African Reserves deepened. The result was seen in the famine of 1960 — the last considered here because thereafter the public records are closed — and probably in the famines which have since become increasingly frequent, culminating in the very severe dearth of 1982-4. Moreover, the famine of 1960 revealed that the settler capitalist economy could no longer handle famine without assistance, because it could no longer absorb the available labour and thereby enable the hungry to purchase food. In 1960, therefore, direct government relief was necessary for the first time since 1922, and this too subsequently became more common. The state filled the widening gaps in the capitalist system of controlling famine mortality, and the system held.

Overall, then, mortality directly due to famine did disappear from Southern Rhodesia in the colonial period, but had seldom been acute at any time. Non-fatal scarcity, on the other hand, remained as common as before. It may even have increased, especially in the late colonial period, but more significantly it changed, especially in its geographical location and social incidence. Similarly, the methods of controlling mortality and relieving need changed greatly, but their efficacy probably remained much the same.

Yet a final qualification must be made. Although it is almost certain that mortality directly due to famine disappeared from Southern Rhodesia during the colonial period, it is still possible that mortality was unusually high in famine years because weakened people became unusually susceptible to ordinary diseases. Mortality of this kind would not have been visible to observers but would have appeared only in mortality statistics, which do not exist for Southern Rhodesia unless mission stations have registers of deaths. The importance of this point was observed in late nineteenth-century India, where the introduction of mortality statistics revealed that deaths in famine years were far more numerous than had hitherto been suspected.[21] If this was true in Southern Rhodesia, then the argument of this book will need major revision.

For the present, however, the first step is to set out the evidence on which the argument rests.

# CHAPTER 2

## Pre-colonial Famine

Pre-colonial Zimbabwe experienced frequent droughts and food shortages. Rainfall statistics suggest that the Shona, the country's main inhabitants for a thousand years, suffer drought in roughly one year in five.[1] Yet evidence that many people died in famine is scarce.

One reason for this lay in the environment. Tropical Africa's rainfall came chiefly from a weather system known as the Inter-Tropical Convergence Zone. This followed the sun northwards and southwards, so that southern tropical regions like Zimbabwe received most of their rainfall between November and March.[2] Other things being equal, the further a tropical region was from the Equator, the shorter and less reliable was its rainy season. Zimbabwe was on the southern edge of the tropics; the Tropic of Capricorn was little over a hundred kilometres south of its southern border. The site of modern Harare was further from the Equator than the notoriously drought-ridden city of Timbuktu in the Sahel of West Africa. Because it was relatively close to the east coast of Africa and its prevailing winds came from that direction, Zimbabwe enjoyed more rain than Timbuktu, whose rain-bearing winds from the south-west had to cross 1 500 kilometres of land. But in another sense Zimbabwe was the Sahel of the South, for it, too, was a region where cultivation without irrigation was possible but never assured, a 'kingdom of uncertainty and anxiety', in words written of another Sahel.[3] 'The same year can never come again', said a Shona proverb,[4] and the rain played cruel tricks on the cultivator: hiding itself until three unsuccessful sowings had exhausted his seed; falling early and copiously to raise splendid crops and then holding off to watch them wither in the sun; or pouring in a torrent to flood the land and rot the grain in the fields. As the dry season dragged wearily into October, men became obsessed by portents, watching the patterns of clouds, the unfurling of leaves, and the behaviour of animals and birds as though nature had foreknowledge. 'The first rain is so longed for, and is preceded by so many signs', the missionary T. M. Thomas wrote of the Ndebele who had settled in the south-west of the country in 1840, 'that those who entirely depend for corn and vegetables upon gardens watered from the clouds, often grow weary and faint-hearted in waiting for it'.[5] Yet this uncertain rainfall, which declined as one moved southwards and came chiefly in showers and thunderstorms, was so localized that a general drought was most

13

exceptional. As another early missionary observed, 'If the crops in one district fail they are good in another'.[6] Local scarcity, therefore, rarely declined into general 'famine that killed'.

Moreover, most of Zimbabwe's peoples minimized the risk of drought by living in relatively favoured environments. A long, narrow plateau of highveld above 1 200 m stretched from south-west to north-east, occupying about one-quarter of the modern country.[7] The plateau's height attracted rainfall, so that the Ndebele in the more arid south-west clustered on it. Shona, however, preferred to exploit the variety of environments available where the highveld merged into the drier middle-veld, between 900 and 1 200 m, which occupies two-fifths of modern Zimbabwe. This explained why all the country's historic kingdoms centred around the edges of the highveld.[8] The remaining one-third of modern Zimbabwe consisted of lowveld, chiefly in the Zambezi, Sabi, Shashi, and Limpopo valleys fringing the country. There were fertile and well-watered tracts even here, but often poor soils enjoyed adequate rainfall only every third or fourth year, so that recurrent scarcity threatened the sparse population.[9] Other ill-favoured environments included the high Inyanga Plateau to the east, whose abundant rain fell on such poor soils that terracing and other special techniques were needed to support agriculture, and the equally infertile sandveld west of the river Gwaai, which merged into the Kalahari. Yet Zimbabwe had none of the purely pastoral people who elsewhere in Africa were especially vulnerable to drought. This was another reason why scarcity rarely degenerated into severe mortality.

The chief defence against scarcity was the cultivator's skill. The staple crops of the Shona were finger millet *(rukweza, rupoko)* and bulrush millet *(mhunga)*. Other grains, legumes, root crops, and a host of vegetables enriched the diet.[10] Soils varied greatly within small areas. Some crops preferred lighter, sandy soils, others the red clays, and preferences differed year by year with the rainfall. The wet alluvial bottoms called vleis were especially valuable defences against drought. Since population was sparse and land freely available, the wise cultivator employed as many combinations of soil and seed as possible in order to provide against all contingencies.[11] Ndebele, too, were mainly cultivators, but the south-western plateau where they lived had less rain and a slightly later harvest, so that they relied more on sorghum *(amabele)* — an early missionary listed fourteen varieties — and bulrush millet *(inyauti)*.[12] Yet each locality had its agricultural specialities. The most distinctive system was that of the Tonga people inhabiting the Zambezi valley, who supplemented their drought-prone grain fields with riverside gardens:

After the Zambezi has been down in flood, which is generally in May, and directly the waters start to subside, the fresh alluvium is assiduously cultivated and followed down foot by foot to the usual water level. Here they plant principally tobacco and maize, the former being as a rule planted first. Each family and each individual of that family has its own little patch neatly fenced off with reeds from that adjoining it and it is a common sight where the banks adjust themselves to the purpose and where there is any considerable population to find mile after mile of what are nothing less than small-holdings, or allotments. These enable the natives practically to be assured of an adequate supply of food for, should the summer crops fail through drought, pests, or some other unforseen reason, the winter crops will carry them through with the addition of edible berries, grasses, etc., in fact a famine on the Zambezi is almost unknown.[13]

Cultivators provided against harvest failure by storing grain, either in the thatched granaries which Shona built on solid rock or in the pits which Ndebele dug beneath cattle kraals. Some accounts suggest that Shona could preserve grain for five years and Ndebele for two,[14] although others quote shorter periods and some cultivators may have maintained only a year's reserve and replaced it with the new harvest.[15] This exposed them to famine if the rains failed in two successive seasons. Should that happen, men relied even more than usual on the fruits, leaves, and roots of the bush, whose importance to the sparse populations of the nineteenth and early twentieth centuries is easily overlooked. European observers often mentioned the small, spherical, orange fruit of the *mahobohobo* or *muzhanje* tree, the wild loquat which crowned the steep kopjes of Shona country, but less conspicuous wild foods were more important. The great experts were the Tonga, whose range of forest produce — one of the widest ever studied in Africa — convinced Livingstone that starvation was impossible in the Zambezi Valley.[16] Women foraged. Men hunted, probably with less reward.[17]

Many other resources prevented scarcity from degenerating into famine mortality. Cattle could be traded or even slaughtered for food. 'In a scarce year', a missionary wrote of the Ndebele, 'they buy corn with oxen, which they kill, cut up and divide out for basketfuls, which they bring for barter' — although only after securing the king's permission to slaughter a beast.[18] The Ndebele king kept large reserves, provided for the poor and needy, and controlled access to the new crops by tasting them at the first-fruits ceremony and then letting the message pass through his country, 'Here is the food: take ye and eat':

Watermelons and sugarcanes, which needed no cooking, were devoured at once. Succulent gourds were cut up, boiled and served out on wooden platters. Mealies were roasted at the fire. The women loosened their girdles, which they had drawn tight round their stomachs to stave off the pangs of hunger. The famished dogs were given their share of the repast. The days of starvation were forgotten.[19]

Shona, too, cultivated fields for their chiefs and instructed them at their accession:

> You are the chief of everyone,
> Father of orphans and of those who suffer.
> Your senior wife,
> Your second wife,
> Your third wife,
> They are to cook for the hungry, serve those who wait for food.[20]

Yet Shona chiefs were relatively small men and the people probably relied more on the large kin-based villages in which they lived, in contrast to the smaller settlements and kin-groups of the Ndebele. Both peoples, however, looked to chiefs and ritualists to secure the lifeblood of rain, so that rain cults — of Leza, Mwari, Dzivaguru, Musikavanhu — were the characteristic religious institutions of the 'kingdom of uncertainty'.[21]

When local resources failed, the hungry scoured the country for grain. Tonga named their famines by the places where they found food. Men from the Sabi valley bartered their salt for food from the highveld. Traders hawked their sparse stocks of imported goods.[22] Fathers pledged their daughters or themselves in return for food — the evidence of bondsmen among the Shona from a very early date suggests a long history of famine.[23] Yet there is little evidence in Zimbabwe (except in times of violence) that scarcity was attended by the epidemic disease which often kills many of those who die in famine. That certainly happened in neighbouring Mozambique, where written records are more numerous and droughts often coincided with those in Zimbabwe, but the smallpox which was the great killer there and elsewhere in pre-colonial Africa, although endemic and carefully treated in late nineteenth-century Zimbabwe, caused neither the alarm nor the mortality which it bred elsewhere.[24]

The actual evidence of famine in Zimbabwe before the mid-nineteenth century comes from oral traditions or Portuguese documents. Both these sources are difficult to use, especially on this subject. The point is illustrated by the country's two earliest recorded subsistence crises. The traditions of the Mutapa kingdom in the middle Zambezi Valley, recorded by Mr D.P. Abraham, state that a great drought took place during the reign following that of the kingdom's founder.[25] Abraham dated this drought somewhere between 1450 and 1480. The tradition says that the Mutapa's victorious followers, who had come from the south, crossed the Zambezi north into Maravi country during the drought, but soon returned. That sounds suspiciously like the concealment of a defeat which brought the northward conquest to an end and settled the kingdom in its subsequent location — but the truth will never be known. The second crisis is said to have occurred in 1561, also in the Mutapa kingdom, following the murder there of the pioneer missionary, Gonçalo da Silveira. One hundred and fifty years later, 'basing himself on a document no longer available to us',[26] a Jesuit historian, Francisco de Sousa, described the catastrophe:

Heaven did not delay in avenging the blood of the just Abel. Immediately there appeared an innumerable and almost infinite army of locusts.... consuming with insatiable hunger everything that the land produced for the sustenance of the miserable people. There followed a terrible plague, which made a pitiful destruction, never seen in Cafraria (South-East Africa). The hunger and the mortality lasted two years.[27]

One must be thankful that Providence is not always so prompt. This famine was not remembered in oral tradition, nor is it mentioned in any surviving contemporary document. It may nevertheless have occurred.

The point is not to deny that serious famine, and perhaps serious famine mortality, occurred in pre-colonial Zimbabwe. It is rather to stress that we have almost no evidence of it. Dr Hoyini Bhila's history of the Manyika region in the east mentions 'frequent outbreaks of famines' in Portuguese times, but Portuguese sources before 1800 seem to refer to the need to import food into the region rather than to famine and suffering.[28] Eighteenth-century traditions from the Sabi valley record a period when 'there was no water and so the people of Nyashanu were drinking the urine of cattle'.[29] No deaths are mentioned.

Yet there was certainly one period of acute and widespread starvation in pre-colonial Zimbabwe. It began during the 1790s with drought and famine in the Manyika region. This initiated many years of anarchy which merged into further droughts and famines in 1827-9 — when thousands are said to have died — and in 1833-6.[30] These calamities were part of a period of dearth throughout the savanna regions of Africa,[31] but in Zimbabwe they were worsened by widespread violence due to invasion by Nguni-speaking groups from South Africa remembered incorrectly as 'Swazi'.[32] Pre-colonial societies were probably less well equipped to survive violence than drought, because violence interrupted the survival procedures like trade and foraging which normally overcame harvest failure. Certainly oral traditions are more explicit about mortality during this crisis than during any other. The 'Swazi' invasion of Maungwe chiefdom in the modern Makoni District of eastern Mashonaland left behind 'a catastrophic period of famine and drought ... remembered still to-day with horror as the "Shangwa"'.[33] In the neighbouring area which became Mrewa District, Chief Mangwende is said to have complained, 'All our country is starving and many people are dying from small-pox. Many people are being killed by the maZungendaba.'[34] The coincidence of violence and drought also caused starvation in the Chibi chiefdom of southern Mashonaland.[35]

The crisis of the early nineteenth century probably included 'famine that killed', but it was almost the last time before 1896 that this could be said with any confidence. When Robert Moffat visited Matabeleland in 1857, for example, he found 'great hunger' as a result of unsatisfactory rains.[36] In 1859 he returned with missionaries who settled in Matabeleland and thereafter kept a continuous written record. They immediately encountered serious food shortage. 'We learned from testimony that the past season had been one of unprecedented drought, supposed to extend as far as the Zambeze', Robert Moffat reported of the winter of 1859.[37] Rain then fell copiously, but scarcity returned in December 1860, before the harvest, 'the poor people living on wild fruits and roots of trees'.[38] When the crops failed early in 1861, serious dearth ensued. 'The hunger is very great', a missionary reported in September. 'We see them going by scores about the country gathering various wild fruits, on which, for the most part, they are subsisting, and must do so until the harvest about April. Many of them travel 80 or 100 miles on foot with a few beads in their hand to buy a bushel or less of corn, from people who are more highly favoured with rains.'[39] The harvest of 1862 also failed and famine extended to the north bank of the Zambezi.[40] 'The Matabele say they have *never* known such seasons as the last three have been', wrote Emily Moffat.[41] Meanwhile traders introduced lung-sickness, which killed thousands of cattle, and smallpox and measles arrived from the south in September 1862, despite attempts to close the border.[42] Reports of famine finally ended late in 1862. And yet at no time between 1857 and 1862 did the missionaries mention a single human death resulting from famine.

Their silence should be compared with a tradition given to a Native Commissioner in the Gutu District of Mashonaland fifty years later:

> About the year 1860, the year known as the 'Musorschena', or 'Shangwa', a very serious famine occurred, when the death rate appears to have been enormous. The natives say that so many people died that they had to be left unburied to be devoured by carrion. During this period it seems that no rain whatever fell, and

during the first favourable season following the drought locusts came and swept the country, causing additional distress. It seems that the drought on this occasion lasted 2 seasons (2 years) and the natives had to exist on roots, etc. This year is one that seems to have affected the country generally, and differs in this respect from other periods of famine that followed.[43]

Famine afflicted the whole of southern Africa during the early 1860s. Missionaries resident in southern Malawi, for example, witnessed heavy mortality in the worst disaster known in that country's history.[44] Yet the missionaries in Matabeleland did not mention a single death. Some must surely have occurred during three years of scarcity. Many could no doubt have happened without the missionaries' knowledge. But it seems unlikely that they could have remained ignorant of anything approaching mass mortality. Nor did they mention deaths in the scarcities which occurred in Matabeleland in 1867, 1872, 1882, 1884, 1887 and 1889.[45]

There were probably three reasons for the missionaries' silence. One is that after the early 1860s there were twenty years of generally good rainfall and crops throughout tropical Africa.[46] Conditions began to deteriorate again during the 1880s, as more frequent scarcity shows, but in general the missionaries observed Matabeleland at a favoured time and were much impressed by its prosperity. The second reason — observed elsewhere in Africa[47] — is that oral traditions and Portuguese documents based upon them probably over-dramatized the past and exaggerated its cataclysmic character, whereas contemporary missionary reports described the banality of daily life. The Jesuit Fathers who visited Matabeleland from 1879, for example, did not once mention famine.[48] The third reason is that serious famine mortality was genuinely very rare in Zimbabwe, whereas the recurrent scarcity which missionaries described was normal. As one put it, 'Famine, though much talked about, is very seldom seen.' 'Hunger is like fibre,' said a Shona proverb; 'it can be removed.'[49] Ndebele traditions scarcely mention famine.

The missionaries were confined to Matabeleland. Evidence from Mashonaland between 1860 and 1890 is fragmentary. Traditions collected in the early twentieth century stated that serious famine mortality occurred in Mangwende's chiefdom in about 1867-8. In the classic manner, it was precipitated by violence and worsened by epidemic:

> Owing to the raids of the Matabili from the west, and the visit from Nyamandi's Shangaans from the east, the people of Noe were having a rather precarious existence. They were unable to cultivate their gardens in safety, and had to subsist on what they could grow in the narrow granite valleys under cover of their strongholds. The two years following the visit

of Nyamandi's army were years of drought; then came the 'Great Famine' in all the eastern districts of Mashonaland. Thousands of people died, and their bones were left to bleach on the veld.

The famine gave a respite from the Matabili raids; but the people were only recovering from the famine when came an outbreak of smallbox which carried off large numbers of the young people.[50]

The next reports of shortage in Mashonaland date from late 1871 and 1872, when Carl Mauch reported hunger near Great Zimbabwe and then found it again more seriously along the Gairesi River which became part of Zimbabwe's border with Mozambique. Since there was scarcity in Matabeleland also at this time, the dearth was widespread and may have included that later remembered in Gutu district as 'Gore rerubayabudzi'.[51] Mangwende's people are said to have suffered another famine in 1879, 'during which many of them died',[52] but the next widespread scarcity, often called 'Gore reMvemve', apparently took place in 1882 and/or 1883; it was probably the dearth attributed by tradition to the killing of the medium of the Chaminuka spirit by the Ndebele king, Lobengula. In the arid Sebungwe district, south of the Zambezi, the scarcity was allegedly so severe that 'women were reduced to eating their skin aprons and many hundreds perished', but deaths are not generally mentioned elsewhere.[53] Local scarcity was reported in the Mazoe valley of northern Mashonaland in 1887,[54] but the last major crisis before colonial invasion occurred in the southern lowveld during 1888-9, when drought and sickness compelled both missionaries and local people to take refuge in higher land, although the published account does not mention deaths.[55]

This scattered evidence from late nineteenth-century Mashonaland suggests that famine was worst when it occurred in the arid lowveld or especially when it was associated with violence. In the latter situation deaths might be numerous.[56] This would support the general picture given in missionary reports from Matabeleland and in earlier records and traditions. Most peoples of pre-colonial Zimbabwe had achieved much control of famine mortality, except when their survival techniques were destroyed by violence.

# CHAPTER 3

## War and Famine, 1896-7

Late in 1896 Matabeleland suffered the worst famine mortality seen anywhere in Zimbabwe since the 'Swazi' invasions. It was a direct result of violence and, therefore, fitted into the pattern of pre-colonial famine history. The Europeans whose violence caused the famine did not admit this. They claimed that the six years since their invasion had witnessed an environmental disaster culminating in 1896, when despairing Africans had blamed their hunger on their rulers and had risen to put an end to both. 'A drought, abnormal alike in its duration and intensity, had set in with the coming of Dr Jameson (to Matabeleland in 1893), and had continued ever since', the British South Africa Company's Administrator, Earl Grey, explained in November 1896. Locusts, he claimed, had appeared in Matabeleland for the first time since 1865, and they were 'locusts of the white man', a more destructive kind than before. In 1896 rinderpest (cattle plague) had arrived to destroy the herds. The prophet of the Mwari cult, Grey claimed, had foretold, 'Until the blood of the white man be spilt, there will be no rain.'[1]

This was greatly exaggerated. The records of the Hope Fountain mission, south of Bulawayo — Zimbabwe's earliest continuous rainfall records — show average rainfall or better in every season between 1889/90 and 1895/6 except 1894/5, when it was only slightly below normal. Salisbury's records are less complete but suggest that only 1891/2 and (less) 1894/5 were below-average seasons. Of course, high annual rainfall did not guarantee a good harvest; that depended also on the distribution of the rain. But the harvests were not unusually bad. Fragmentary reports from Matabeleland suggest that grain was abundant in 1890 but scarcer in 1891, when the rains, although copious, were late and destructive.[2] By January 1892 there was 'a good deal of hunger' around Hope Fountain, partly owing to the arrival of locusts — a plague throughout tropical Africa during the 1890s — which had last been reported in 1871.[3] But there were no subsequent reports of shortage in Matabeleland until early 1894, when they resulted from the European invasion of October 1893, the withdrawal of the main Ndebele forces northwards, and the flight of many civilians. Both missionaries and the Company aided hungry people at this time and vaccinated many against smallpox. Yet the rains of 1893/4 were excellent, most crops were planted normally, and the harvest appears to have sufficed until the end of 1894.[4] Severe shortages were reported in Matabeleland early in 1895, but late rains saved the crops and 1895 was in general quite a good year, despite below-average rainfall.[5] In Mashonaland, by contrast, 1895 saw the first really bad harvest since the British invasion, owing to drought and locusts. By September 1895 some villages were wholly dependent on wild produce and the collection of tax had to be suspended, although certain districts had surplus grain to exchange. More representative was the Afrikaner settler in Melsetter who wrote in February 1896, 'We cannot barter any more food from the natives, because they have nothing, the locusts having destroyed it all.'[6]

The notion that harvest failure in 1896 — coinciding with the arrival of rinderpest in February or March — was a proximate cause of revolt was an important element in the British South Africa Company's apologia. Yet Salisbury and Hope Fountain both enjoyed slightly above-average rainfall in 1895/6. Since Shona did not rebel until June 1896, when their harvest was completed, it is known that their crops were generally good, except in the Sabi valley and where locusts were exceptionally active.[7] Ndebele, by contrast, rebelled before the harvest and predictions of its quality fluctuated from 'dismal' and 'forlorn' to 'not bad at all' and even 'splendid'.[8] In the event, Ndebele crops varied even more than usual from one locality to another. They failed in the Bubi District to the north of Bulawayo, in the Solusi area to the west, and perhaps partly in the Empandeni and Matopos areas to the south-west.[9] To the south-east of Bulawayo, however, they were excellent in the Filabusi and Insiza Districts and especially in Umzingwane, whose Native Commissioner reported in September 1896:

> In my district the last season was a good one though in the higher parts of the District much harm was done to the crops by locusts and drought. In the lower parts and especially in the large and fertile valley of the Umzingwane River the crops standing and ready for reaping at the time of the outbreak were exceptionally good and at the same time some of the kraals had still on hand a considerable amount of corn over from the preceding season, notably the Engrabeweni Kraal where the corn pits were almost full. I have no hesitation in saying that if the rebellion had not broken out the Natives in my district would have had more than sufficient corn for their own use — quite enough in fact to trade largely.[10]

On balance, it seems unlikely that 1896 would have been a famine year purely as a result of the harvest. Rinderpest certainly robbed the people of a major famine reserve and perhaps prevented certain individuals whose crops had failed from obtaining grain by exchanging stock. After their conquest of Matabeleland in 1893 the Europeans had in any case seized most Ndebele cattle and smaller numbers from Shona. From 1894 the newly-formed Native Department demanded tax and labour.[11] This may have exposed individuals to want, but was probably not sufficiently widespread to cause extensive famine. The same was true of land alienation. Almost the whole highveld nucleus of the Ndebele kingdom was seized by Europeans after 1893, two remote and arid Native Reserves were demarcated, and some Ndebele moved to the fringes of the state, but in 1895 only 150 of the 1 070 European farms in Matabeleland were worked, so that many Ndebele remained on their former land, not yet paying rent but sometimes supplying labour on demand.[12] Because Shona lived in scattered hilltop settlements, European farms seldom dispossessed them except in the Melsetter area, where Afrikaners appropriated almost all the highveld and exacted labour with much brutality. Elsewhere, European demand positively stimulated Shona production.[13]

In general, then, the famine of 1896 was not due to six years of natural catastrophe, a single disastrous drought, or European intrusion as such. It was created by the violence of the rebellion and its suppression, just as pre-colonial famines that killed had been caused by violence. The rebellion began in Matabeleland on 20 March, perhaps prematurely, for although Ndebele leaders were certainly planning revolt, they may well have intended to wait until May or June, after the harvest.[14] Once violence began, however, Ndebele moved their women and children, their surviving stock, and the grain stores remaining from the harvest of 1895 to strongholds in the Matopos Hills and other retreats. By holding the Europeans on the defensive in Bulawayo during April and the first half of May, Ndebele harvested and stored some standing crops, as European troops found when they penetrated the Matopos during August:

> We found very large stores of grain here, packed in immense neatly-woven grass baskets made with a small mouth which was sealed up with mortar; there were mealies (maize), inyaooti (Kaffir corn), monkey-nuts, rice, dried melons, and Mahoba-hoba fruit, etc., these were all stored in large, dry caves, of which the entrances had been stockaded.[15]

Much was still in the fields, however, when European patrols began to regain the initiative during May. 'Food is very scarce this year', a missionary wrote from Hope Fountain on 5 June, 'and there will be much suffering among the natives on this account. Most of the grain is finished all round about this district. The enemy come out of the hills to gather as much as they can.'[16] To prevent them from harvesting was a vital military objective for the Company. 'All native supplies of corn are destroyed throughout the eastern districts where the war has raged and in the west drought and locusts have spoilt the crops', another missionary reported on 19 July.[17] Five days later his colleague pointed to a new threat. 'The digging season is coming on and hunger is telling upon the women and children', he wrote, 'and they most of them are anxious to return to dig their gardens but if the indunas refuse the war may drag on all through the rainy season wh(ich) will soon be upon us'.[18]

By August both sides faced a crisis. The Ndebele had lost the initiative, they were running short of food, groups were beginning to fight one another for the remaining supplies, and they faced the fundamental problem of living 'within a society whose economy demanded the resolution of conflict every spring'.[19] Yet the Europeans, too, faced a crisis. Late in July their newly-arrived Imperial troops advanced towards the Matopos Hills, met sharp resistance, and halted on the edge of terrain superbly suited to guerrilla warfare. While the Imperial commander contemplated reinforcements, the Company — which was paying for the troops and feared that the Imperial authorities might supersede it — contemplated negotiations with Ndebele leaders. Famine became the core of the Company's strategy. Troops in the Matopos shouted to their Ndebele enemies on nearby hills, 'Why are your crops not sown yet?'[20] Rhodes stressed famine at his indaba with Ndebele chiefs on 28 August: 'The rains are close upon us, and the time for ploughing your gardens and sowing is short. If it is to be peace, prove that you really mean it by sending your women and children and come out yourselves into your gardens and sow them before it is too late.'[21] Within days unarmed men and women were cultivating the valleys and this news was encouraging surrender in the west and north-west of Matabeleland, where harvest failure made starvation especially acute.[22] In the Shangani area the seizure of supplies had become the chief military objective:

> The camp has settled down to a steady business in the way of grain collecting which has now become one of the principle duties of the day. The natives who have surrendered are used as carriers to save the mules. After breakfast a long string of them of both sexes and all ages may be seen wending their way to some Mashona kraal perched on a granite kopje. The 'Isipalla' or grain bins are emptied into baskets by the men and carried down to the bottom of the hill. The women place them on their heads and carry them back to camp, where they are emptied into a large reservoir. Here the corn is put into sacks and stacked in readiness for removing by wagon. About 400 sacks have been brought in from within a radius of two miles from our camp, besides feeding from 1000 to 1200 friendlies and prisoners, 27 spans of mules and

a number of horses. So far so good. We have spoiled the Mad-waleiners. We have got them out of their strongholds and taken away their corn.[23]

Famine was also the Company's lever to oust the Imperial troops and their ambitious commanders. Since rinderpest ruled out ox-wagon transport from the railhead at Mafeking, 940 km away, the price of maize meal in Bulawayo had soared from an already high £4 a bag in March 1896 to about £13 in October.[24] Not only did this raise the cost of supplying troops, but the shortage of transport meant that the food they and their horses consumed could be presented as food denied to starving Africans. 'Policy of insisting upon keeping in country during rains unnecessarily large force means unnecessary starvation natives', Grey telegraphed on 11 October.[25] The tactic worked. Within six weeks the Imperial commander was reporting 'that there is no further occasion for Military operations'.[26] And famine offered another advantage. 'As soon as the natives have got their seed in the ground and are in sight of harvest', Grey explained during November, 'it will be within the power of the Administration to take such action as may be necessary to obtain a surrender of arms'.[27]

As early as 19 August a captive taken in the Matopos Hills declared that many women and children had already died for want of food.[28] During the next five months starvation slowly engulfed the Ndebele. It was least severe in the east, where the harvest had been good, rinderpest was least destructive, and there was relatively little fighting. Both Insiza and Belingwe Districts reported in December 1896 that supplies would suffice until the new harvest.[29] Elsewhere, during the last months of 1896, women laboured 'from sunrise to sundown' to sow a grain crop, either in the previous year's fields or in small plots in the mountain valleys and forest retreats where they had taken refuge.[30] The fighting men, by contrast, depended increasingly on plunder. Some regiments raided one another's stores. Others pillaged 'friendlies', especially in the west. 'The friendlies in this district are very hard up for grain', the Chief Native Commissioner reported in November from Bulalima. 'Many of them had their crops raided by the rebels in the first instance, others again suffered owing to the drought and locusts.'[31] Looted also by White troops, these 'friendlies' often suffered severely from famine. Yet the greatest violence and misery was in the north, where largely undefeated regiments withdrew through drought- and locust-ridden country towards the Zambezi, battening on subject peoples and forest-dwellers. 'The Matabili have completely scattered all the "rolis" (subjects) in the country north of Manyeu's kraal through which we passed', a Native Commissioner reported in March 1897, 'they have plundered them of food, arms, seed

25

and goods often illtreating them and are now living in their kraals. We came upon a few of these wretched people wandering about and looking for roots etc. and a few watching last years gardens.'[32] Many victims sought refuge across the Zambezi. After exhausting local food stores, warriors turned their guns on the game, some surviving independently in this way as late as August 1898.[33]

Foraging skills were never more valuable:

> Some natives are starving having to eat baboons and monkeys, others grind up the skins of rinderpest oxen and cook the powder for food, while others are now living on wild fruit such as berries, and roots of trees in the veldt. Many appeal to me for food now they don't pat their stomacks while speaking of being hungry, but say, 'Look at my body, my arms, my legs, I am just like a rugged koppie, am all corners ...' Fancy some of them selling their children for food. One of my most promising girls is to be given away according to native custom for corn.[34]

'On the banks of the Shangani there are a good many people who are living on the pith of the palm trees', a Native Commissioner reported in February 1897. 'This pith is not unpalatable and contains a lot of vegetable oil, it tastes much like sweet potatoes.'[35] Others survived on roots or dried melon slices. 'We passed several natives cutting the best pieces off the bodies of dead rinderpest oxen which have been lying there decaying for *months'*, Lady Grey wrote to her son in October 1896.[36] Such food bred sickness in weakened people. James Mkiza described those surrendering at Nyamandhlovu:

> The rebels are in a horrible state of starvation, and are suffering from a disease, which I believe is caused through eating Rinderpest rotten skins, and wild roots, the effect of which causes them to purge considerably. During the time I was there the rebels lived on the dry skins they picked up on the veldt, they also lived on old dry water-melons... Syphilis is also amongst the rebels to a considerable extent, and they admit that they are unable to cure it.[37]

Others reported deaths from fever, but no epidemic occurred. Two smallpox cases were diagnosed and isolated in Bulawayo during December 1896, but the disease did not spread.[38]

Compared with the contribution made by foraging, the Company's relief efforts were slender but useful where so many were close to death. As starving people began to surrender during September, local commanders fed them from captured stocks. On 1 October the Chief Native Commissioner opened a distribution centre in Bulawayo.[39] Eight days later Rhodes — doubtless anxious to improve his public image and remove the Imperial troops — pressed the authorities to import grain, offering to guarantee £50 000 from his own funds.[40] Long delay ensued while mule wagons trundled slowly up from Mafeking, but by the end of the Ndebele rebellion nearly one million pounds of grain had been distributed — little enough when compared with the estimated 113 200 surviving people in Matabeleland in 1897, but transport from the railhead alone had cost £50 000.[41] Officials impressed the point on Ndebele chiefs:

> The government are doing all they can, and though hunger moves more quickly over the veldt than the wagons of the Company, we intend to keep as many of them alive as possible.... As you have well said, there is much hunger among your people, and it is now that you turn to the white man to help you in your need. We might easily say to you 'there is corn in Matabeleland why don't you go to your own people and not come to us?' But those are not our words and we have shewn you the clemency which is the child of our great strength.... We have kept our word; we have given you peace and have allowed you to come out of the hills to sow your gardens. Were your words false? If not, where are your arms?[42]

Since there were no vehicles to carry food to the districts, the hungry had to fetch it. Bulawayo saw a flood of starving people into town for the only time in Zimbabwe's history. At its peak in December 1896 the office of the Chief Native Commissioner, H. J. Taylor, was distributing food to nearly 3 000 people each day. A very large proportion were women. They came especially from the west and north of Matabeleland. Many were 'mere skeletons'.[43] 'Scarcely a day passes even now', a local newspaper reported in February, 'that the bodies of dead natives are not picked up on the veld near the town, the victims of starvation'.[44] That some hundreds of girls sold themselves as prostitutes or concubines caused public scandal, but the crowds were passive and it was not until January that the European public — later so critical of free handouts — objected to this largess. While continuing to supply the elderly, women, and children freely, the authorities then set able-bodied males to scavenging and road-making or supplied them to private employers.[45]

Taylor's office ceased to issue food on 15 February 1897, claiming that sufficient wild produce had become available to keep people alive. In general that was probably true. The rains had begun in November and were slightly above average. Crops were patchy but generally satisfactory. The chief danger was locusts, whose depredations — reinforced, no doubt, by many people's hunger — led cultivators to harvest in April, some weeks earlier than usual. Only in the lowveld of Tuli District on the south-western border did the harvest fail. 'The natives of this District are in a starving condition....', the Native Commissioner reported in June:

27

From here to the Mzingwane River every land I came across was
stripped perfectly bare by the locusts, and from the Mzingwane to
the Bubye they have not had a drop of rain this season. The consequence is that the corn is only standing 4 feet high now and only
just coming into ear, from which lands they will of course reap
nothing. Only a very few of the people have managed to get even
melons to eat this year. They are simply living on palm-nuts,
cream of tartar and various roots and berries. Very few of them
have any stock either, it mostly having died of rinderpest. In conclusion I think I can safely say that in the 200 miles I travelled (there
and back) that there is not a single native who will get a bucket of
corn out of his lands this year. The general cry in the District
when you ask for labour is that the men have all gone away in
search of food from the more fortunate natives.[46]

Elsewhere in Matabeleland, however, the crops were gathered by the
middle of 1897, a degree of order returned, and it was possible to count
the cost. The losses were worst in the north, where the harvest of 1895/6
had failed and regiments had plundered whatever existed. Gielgud, the
27-year-old American who was Native Commissioner at Inyati, reported
deaths from starvation in the west of his district at the end of October
1896. A month later they were numerous. By January the famine was
'very terrible' and whole families were dying.[47] During the next two months
he moved his headquarters further northwards towards the Shangani,
where many hard-core rebels had taken refuge and conditions were
worst. 'Sickness is still very prevalent throughout the District and many
deaths have occurred during the month', Gielgud reported early in April
1897:

The cause of death in most cases is fever. The prevalence of fever
this year even among people inhabiting old kraals is very great,
and I think attributable to there being no cattle to keep the grass
down, and which is particularly rank this year. I estimate that
nearly one fourth of the population of this District have died since
the beginning of the rebellion, from wounds, hunger and disease
....The rainfall this year has been quite up to the average and if it
were not for the presence of large numbers of locusts the crops
would have been satisfactory. However owing to these insects the
crops in many parts have been almost entirely destroyed. The
people who have suffered most are those who were backward in
surrendering, for the people who surrendered first planted early
and their crops were already big when the locusts appeared in
large numbers.[48]

A year later Gielgud reported that locusts had again destroyed the crops
in this area and the population had further decreased.[49] Nowhere else
were losses on this scale suggested, but deaths from starvation and

disease were reported from all corners of Matabeleland: 'many deaths' from fever and famine in Mzingwane District to the south-east of Bulawayo; over thirty by the end of 1896 at the Hope Fountain mission to the south; and some hundreds, it appears, at Empandeni mission in the extreme south-west.[50] As in most 'famines that kill', deaths appear to have been most numerous among the old, who, unlike women and children, could not journey to Bulawayo. 'The people who suffer most are the old men and women', a Native Commissioner wrote from Shiloh, north of Bulawayo; 'these old people are living alone at their kraals eiking (sic) out a miserable existance while the young men are away north and the women are seeking work away from home.'[51] No estimate of total mortality is possible, but it was unquestionably the most terrible that Southern Rhodesia experienced.

Mashonaland, although the war continued longer there, suffered less from famine. Indeed, the Shona were more difficult to repress not only because they lacked overall leaders but because they were more difficult to starve. Their methods of storing grain were superior to those of the Ndebele, they had more experience of hiding their reserves from foraging enemies, and unlike the Ndebele they delayed their rebellion until June 1896, after the harvest. Within a few weeks Europeans regained the offensive and began to destroy those stores they could find. 'About six weeks after the outbreak', the Native Commissioner in Salisbury recalled, 'I loaded up five or six wagons with grain at Mashonganyika's kraal and burnt the remainder'.[52] By the time Imperial troops reached Salisbury on 25 August, however, Shona were already preparing their fields for the new season. Although active in destroying stores where Europeans had been killed or overt resistance continued,[53] the authorities despised the Shona as fighters, believed they wanted peace, and were not eager to create another famine. 'All who are willing to sow their crops should be allowed to do so, provided they adopt no hostile attitude whatever', the Chief Native Commissioner recommended in December.[54] The Administrator agreed, believing that growing crops would encourage surrender. 'I think you quite understand the policy which the Administration wishes to pursue towards the natives', he told an agent. '... After the seed is in the ground the Administration can press for the surrender of both arms and murderers. You will know how to deal with the subject.'[55] Through the summer of 1896-7, therefore, Shona were mostly left to cultivate in peace. Dissidents were occasionally raided. There were pockets of scarcity on the highveld and both famine and smallpox in the arid Sabi valley.[56] At Salisbury the rainfall was 115 mm below normal, but locusts were less destructive than in recent years. In general, the crops were good. The military commissariat reported that transport, not grain, was scarce.[57]

By mid-February 1897, therefore, the authorities had still not subdued most parts of central Mashonaland, guns had not been surrendered, and it was too late to destroy more than a fraction of the standing crops. Chiefs such as Mashayamombe were temporizing in the hope of gathering the harvest before hostilities began. Early in March, as the drying countryside made movement easier, the authorities began to destroy crops systematically in dissident areas, starting in the Mazoe valley. This campaign put great pressure on some hard-core rebels but did not prevent the major chiefs from replenishing their stores. When Nyandoro's stronghold was finally taken in June 1897, for example, it contained masses of grain in newly-constructed bins.[58] The capture of Mashayamombe's capital on 24 July was the last major action of the war. With the need to prepare their fields once more imminent, most surviving rebels surrendered during the following weeks, although the spirit-medium of Nehanda was not captured until December.

'The efforts failed and the action that followed caused us tremendous hardship', a Shona headman later recalled:

> We fled into the hills to escape punishment. Women carried children in huge baskets balanced on their heads, several infants in one basket, whilst in their arms they carried supplies. Men and boys helped carry grain, pots and other essentials to their hiding places and livestock was driven before the fleeing Africans. Hinga, we more than paid for the uprising![59]

Everywhere, so the Company reported, the Shona rebel areas were much impoverished.[60] 'The people were in a wretched condition, a state of semi-starvation, living chiefly on berries and roots', a missionary reported in September 1897 from Zvimba's country to the west of Salisbury. 'I have never seen more miserable specimens of humanity.'[60] Yet there was no 'famine that killed' to match that in northern and western Matabeleland. The Shona people had once more survived.

# CHAPTER 4

## Famine along the Rivers, 1903

During 1903 Southern Rhodesia experienced a drought and food shortage of a kind which had probably occurred repeatedly, although often less severely, before colonial rule.[1] On the highveld a single harvest failure produced widespread scarcity. In the arid lowlands along the rivers, especially where previous seasons had been poor, there was serious starvation and a mortality which is now difficult to assess. The interest of this famine is its close resemblance to those of the past. It was not a transitional famine with elements of both pre-capitalist and capitalist crises. Although White settlers had formally appropriated at least one-sixth of Southern Rhodesia's land,[2] chiefly on the highveld, this contributed little to the famine, except perhaps in Melsetter District. Instead, the famine centred in those districts least affected by the colonial invasion and transport system. Moreover, the hungry relied overwhelmingly on the survival techniques of the past, which retained all their effectiveness. There were, of course, new elements in the situation. The Native Commissioner distributing grain brought by railway and ox-wagon was one actor on the stage in 1903. But he had only a minor role. The leading actors were from an older world.

The famine came after five generally favourable years. Locusts did much damage in the late 1890s but were disappearing by 1902. Salisbury enjoyed at least 100 mm more than its average rainfall in every year between 1898/9 and 1901/2. Bulawayo was less fortunate, but the first two years of the twentieth century were prosperous there as well. Apart from a few local shortages and a serious dearth in the Zambezi valley in 1899,[3] there was no widespread scarcity once the effects of the rebellion passed — certainly nothing to compare with the terrible famines in East Africa in 1897-1900 and in Mozambique in 1900-2[4].

These were prosperous years for African cultivators. It is true that by 1903 colonial maps showed central Matabeleland almost entirely appropriated by White estates and fringed by 16 Native Reserves, while Mashonaland was a patchwork of European farms and 80 Native Reserves. On the ground, however, things were different. Even in 1904 only 301 farms were occupied by White men. Four years earlier it was estimated, most unreliably, that Europeans farmed only 1 per cent of the grain acreage cultivated by Africans.[5] Admittedly, the emphasis was shifting as Europeans realized that Southern Rhodesia was no Witwatersrand. It was in 1903 that the British South Africa Company began

31

seriously to encourage White farming. Some European landowners demanded rent from the Africans who still often occupied their land, sometimes provoking them to move to the Reserves.[6] Generally, however, the colony's agriculture was still in African hands, as became clear when the scarcity of 1903 deterred them from selling their grain. 'It is hardly a bright reflection on the state of (European) agriculture', a settler newspaper commented, 'to note that so soon as the kafir trade in this commodity fails customers have to take the imported article'.[7]

For five years before 1903 African cultivators prospered by supplying European demands. Fort Victoria District in Southern Mashonaland was the Mecca for grain traders:

> The Kopje country, the native districts to the east and south-east, are as fertile as the high-veld is barren. As a rule, the natives had an immense quantity of surplus grain for sale to traders, in fact they had begun to grow it for sale, working very hard in their fields during the Summer and Autumn, although, officially, they were.... a wickedly lazy people....
>
> The traders on the out-stations bought the grain, paying for it entirely with goods — blankets, limbo (cloth), hoes, beads, and salt being the principal articles given. It was then ridden into Victoria, the middleman usually sending out the wagons to fetch it; and then forwarded as a rule in other wagons, to the Selukwe mines....
>
> There were all sorts of queer little wagons and spans working between the outside traders' camps and the township. Some were owned by natives, some by coolies, though, in the majority of cases, they belonged to the poorer class of Afrikanders.[8]

Charter District in central Mashonaland was another granary, as was Makoni District further east. Their counterparts in Matabeleland were Belingwe and Bulalima. The favoured crop for sale in both regions was maize, hitherto grown less than millet but now preferred for labour rations.[9] In Matabeleland a few hundred cultivators acquired ploughs and some wealthy Chiefs bought wagons and took to transport riding. Cattle herds slowly recovered. Unreliable figures showed that between 1897-8 and 1904 the cattle in African hands in Mashonaland increased from 9 295 to 76 220 and in Matabeleland from 4 688 to 29 190. Prices were very high: six bags of grain for a Mashona bull in Charter District in June 1903.[10]

It was, therefore, against a background of prosperity and the excellent crops of 1901/2[11] that men on the highveld endured the exceptional heat and fickle rains of the summer of 1902/3. On 3 January 1903 a newspaper predicted the worst crops since the rebellion. During the remainder of the month nearly 300 mm of rain fell at Chishawasha, near

Salisbury. Forecasts grew more hopeful. In February Chishawasha enjoyed less than 40 mm. Gloom returned.[12] Then late but localized rains in March shook the kaleidoscope once more. The outcome was extraordinarily patchy. In Gutu maize failed but finger-millet prospered; in Hartley it was exactly the reverse.[13] Generally, however, the highveld harvest was a partial failure. Both Salisbury and Bulawayo registered their worst rainfall since records had begun: only 64 and 76 per cent of the average respectively.

As winter closed over the highveld, men turned to their customary means of supplementing their crops. They drove their sheep and goats from the drought-stricken north of Mrewa District to barter for grain in favoured regions. In Hartley some bought from European traders, but few sold as in prosperous seasons. Many prepared the land for an early crop: 'There is scarcely a valley (in Makoni District) where the native is not (to) be seen up to his knees in muck, turning over the damp sod for early mealies.'[14] By September the price of grain had risen so steeply that many could afford to buy only their seed, surviving meanwhile on roots, baobab fruits, an exceptionally heavy crop of wild plums, or the locusts which were now 'a merciful dispensation'.[15] October saw increased movement as men sought out relatives who still had supplies. By then, however, all eyes were on the clouds and those who controlled them. 'As usual, at this time of the year, rain makers and the disciples of the native God (Mhondoro or Mlimo) are reaping a golden harvest in presents and tithes', the Native Commissioner reported from Hartley.[16] Mwari was propitiated. Rain fell copiously in Mashonaland during November, although Matabeleland had to wait until January and there was everywhere a grim delay while new crops matured. Thefts multiplied, children hungered, but Native Commissioners on the highveld insisted that there was no starvation.[17] They were probably wrong. In prosperous Charter District the missionary Arthur Shearly Cripps, newly arrived but closer to the people than most Europeans, recorded his first horrified experience of famine and mourned the scattering of deaths around him:

> Gray-heads twain and breast-babes three! Ye that might not stay
> Till the green sheaths ruddied and the white gems grew![18]

Yet the highveld escaped lightly. The famine of 1903 concentrated its misery in the distant valleys of the Sabi, Lundi, and Zambezi. Conditions in the Sabi valley and its many tributaries had probably been worsened by an influx of refugees from the neighbouring highlands, where Afrikaner settlers had appropriated land and labour with great brutality.[19] This may have put pressure on the lowveld's scanty resources, especially during drought. Unlike the plateau, the Sabi valley had reaped poor crops during 1902. When the rains failed again in February 1903 nearly 4 000 of its inhabitants were left without grain or the hope of a harvest for more than twelve months. On 14 February Native Commissioner Meredith in Melsetter warned the government to hold 5 000 bags of relief grain in readiness.[20] Yet the valley dwellers were great survivors. 'In many places the Natives are cultivating in damp places and turning water on by means of small furrows in the hope of raising some vegetables and early mealies', Meredith reported in April. '....All the Natives who are short of food are sending their young men out to work.'[21] In June he inspected granaries in the valley and found them entirely empty. 'The Natives are buying food on the high country and are making salt for barter', he wrote; 'many are living on the seeds and fruit of the baobab trees and other edible fruits and roots.'[22] Similar conditions reigned further west along the Lundi. By September the valley people were slaughtering stock to exchange for grain wherever it could be found. In November came the only account of deaths in the southern lowveld during 1903. 'Reports from the lower parts of the District', the Native Commissioner wrote from Chibi, 'state that the Shangaan population of those parts have left their kraals and gone into other Districts in search of food; some 2 or 3 natives have also died of starvation.'[23] There the crops of 1903/4 were again bad. So they also threatened to be on the Sabi in January 1904, when the people were 'absolutely starving',[24] but a month later the prospects improved and the worst of the crisis was over.

Further north, the Tonga and their neighbours in the middle Zambezi valley were already living on bush produce when 1903 began. Four months later it was clear that the crops had again failed. Men climbed the escarpment to buy sorghum from their southern neighbours for £1 a bag. By August some were dying.

> In the belt of country lying between the Zambesi River and forty miles south, and along it for a distance of 200 miles it has been reported that the Natives are subsisting entirely on roots, as they reaped no crops at all last season, with a few exceptions. Dandawa, one of the Paramounts in this part of the district, reports that three people have died of starvation. The deaths are caused most likely from disease induced by having to eat all sorts of roots to keep life and limb together. Nematombo, another Paramount in the same part and lying considerably to the West of Dandawa, came in to report that his people were scattered all over the veldt looking for roots etc, and that he would be unable to pay his tax.[25]

Visiting the valley early in September, the Native Commissioner from Lomagundi found starvation everywhere, especially among Dandawa's people. 'Some of the men and women are very thin indeed', he reported, 'and a few are little more than walking skeletons. All the children are

34

pitifully thin.'[26] In this region September usually brought a harvest in the riverside gardens won from the falling Zambezi, but this year the flood was so low and the gardens so small that by November hunger was returning:

> Rumours of children dying in the North Eastern part of the District from starvation have reached me, but have not been confirmed by direct report. The Natives living in the 'starvation' area are looking fairly well and in fair condition. The children and the older women seem to be the sufferers by shortage of food. The women do most of the hard work in connection with the preparing of the various wild fruits, beans etc, on which they are subsisting.[27]

Further upriver, the Native Commissioner in Wankie reported total crop failure, suffering, and starvation.[28] His colleague in Sebungwe echoed this:

> The percentage of deaths has been higher than usual, no doubt caused by the people being reduced to a low condition of health by famine and in consequence unable to withstand frequent attacks of malarial fever and pneumonia — the two latter maladies being always present throughout the Zambesi Valley.[29]

At the end of the year, however, good rains fell in the valley. Patrolling there again in January 1904, Lomagundi's Native Commissioner heard many complaints of hunger and news of two further deaths, but there were many green vegetables and the maize stood above his head on horseback.[30] The crisis was over for another year.

Further down the valley, however, it was still acute. Here the highlands of the North Mazoe (later Mount Darwin) District fell precipitously into the Dande, the arid plains bordering Mozambique and the Zambezi. It was the most remote place in the whole colony. Between 1901 and 1910 nine different junior officials administered it.[3] In June 1903 the current Assistant Native Commissioner, H.C.K. Fynn — later dismissed for flogging Africans[32] — reported laconically, 'Some relief to the natives of the N.E. would be welcomed by them, they practically had no harvest, and the Portuguese have since visited them.'[33] As suffering grew, however, so did his compassion. 'The natives are in a very bad condition at present, on account of want of food', he wrote early in September. 'The district is a desert with the exception of the Mazoe and Ruia River valleys, the natives have built temporary kraals along the banks and are living on fish and Baobab nuts'.[34] Almost as he wrote, starvation and military harrassment at last forced the Shona chief Mapondera to surrender after nine years of resistance, deliberately sacrificing himself so that his people could cultivate.[35] In October Fynn patrolled the Dande:

What were strongly running streams a few months ago, are now dry watercourses with stagnant pools at long intervals. Even the great Ruia River is reduced to silent shallow reaches. At most of the Kraals the natives are in a state of semi-starvation.... Their principal food at present consists of wild fruit of various sorts, tree-nuts and fish. The adult male natives manage to thrive on this scanty fare, but it comes very hard on the women and children.... I visited six Kraals in the Eastern portion of the District, and saw signs of starvation at all.[36]

Rain began to fall in North Mazoe on 9 November and Fynn supplied seed where needed. Huge areas were cultivated. But the crisis continued for several months until the harvest. Men from the Dande flocked into the highlands, seeking employment with more fortunate Africans, bringing their sheep and goats to trade, offering even their daughters:

In the year 1904.... Munaba came to me at Charamba's kraal in this district saying he was starving and would betroth his daughter to me if I gave him grain. I agreed and gave him a load, he went home and came back with a lot of people and took away a bin of grain.[37]

In February even Chief Kanyera died 'from general debility, his death being accelerated by privations he had suffered during the past year'.[38] Fynn again patrolled the Dande:

Their sufferings from want of food during the past year are most manifest, and at the time of my visit they were still in a deplorable condition. This was more apparent amongst the women and children, who were very emaciated. Until the Munga (bulrush millet) is reaped their principal article of food will be grass seed, which they pound into flour, and then with the addition of water, make into a paste, which is then eaten. The nourishing properties of this diet appear to be very small and just sufficient to prolong life. These people have planted very large areas of Munga, which is in excellent condition and gives promise of a very large yield.[39]

The harvest began in March 1904. 'The famine', Fynn reported, 'may be said to be now at an end'.[40]

Total mortality during the famine of 1903 cannot be estimated. Not a single European lived in the areas worst affected. Assuming that only a small proportion of deaths were known to Native Commissioners, perhaps some hundreds may have died, chiefly along the rivers but also, as Cripps's evidence suggests, small numbers on the highveld. Many of the deaths were probably due to an epidemic of the relatively mild form of smallpox — known to contemporary Europeans as 'Kaffirpox' — which was almost endemic in Southern Rhodesia. The epidemic began in Ndanga District in the south-east, where the Native Commissioner reckoned that 6 or 7 per cent of those infected died.[41] His neighbour in Melsetter took it calmly:

> Smallpox does not appear to be much feared by the Natives; the majority of them have had it or have been inoculated with virus taken direct from a patient suffering from smallpox.
> I have known Natives to recover from an attack of this kind of smallpox after five days illness; they have their faces deeply marked with the prints. Others have been so deeply marked that loss of sight has been the result.[42]

Inoculation during previous epidemics generally meant that only children contracted the disease. Native Commissioners ordered headmen to isolate those infected, destroy their huts, and prevent communication between infected and uninfected villages. A lay official — usually a police trooper — then toured the villages with a supply of lymph to vaccinate all those not previously inoculated. He rarely met resistance. Some 80 000 people were vaccinated in this way during 1903.[43] From Ndanga the epidemic spread through the lowveld and then northwards into Gutu, Selukwe, and Charter Districts. Reporting several deaths, the Native Commissioner in Gutu explained, 'The Natives in this part are very short of food and a strict quarantine could not be enforced unless the Government is prepared to supply the Natives in quarantine with food'.[44] Meredith pointed to the same link with famine in Melsetter: 'it is almost impossible to control the movements of the Native during a season like the present'.[45] Not until February 1904 did the epidemic in Ndanga begin to decline. Medical reports do not suggest numerous deaths,[46] but this was probably the most serious epidemic to accompany any twentieth-century famine in Southern Rhodesia.

Vaccination against smallpox was probably the government's most effective way of controlling mortality in 1903. Its ability to supply relief had certainly increased greatly since the desperate last months of 1896, especially when the railway reached Bulawayo in 1897, and Salisbury in 1899. As one official reported, 'Very large numbers of natives came in to Umtali daily and bought rice, which was obtainable at a very moderate figure, owing to the action of the Railway in the reduction of rates on imported grain, and of the Government in allowing its importation free of duty.'[47] Several Native Commissioners established stocks of grain early in 1903. 'Had not the Government assisted the natives with grain', the Chief Native Commissioner in Mashonaland reflected, 'I feel sure that the number of deaths from starvation would have been large.'[48] Yet in many areas hungry men showed no interest in the government's proffered relief. The Native Commissioner in Salisbury disposed of only two of the

37

bags of grain he had so carefully stocked. Chief Dandawa in the Zambezi valley refused an offer of food even at the height of the famine, 'because he said he had no money for the current tax, and that he would not be able to meet this liability, when added to the current tax'.[49] Cost was the main objection to official relief. As soon as famine threatened, the settler press insisted that the free issues of 1896-7 should not be repeated:

> We trust that the authorities will not be handing hundreds of bags of grain to the natives free, as was done before. The natives will be able to get all the food that they want both for themselves and their wives if they care to work for it, and any charity only tends to keep them in idleness. We expect that we shall hear terrible stories of starving women and children, but we are accustomed to those yarns, which are only weapons with which to browbeat the settlers and the Government and arouse the animosity of the people at Home. There must be no pandering to this kind of terrorism, and if the natives want grain they must pay full market price for it. There may be an attempt to palliate this by granting the natives seed grain. We think that this would also be a mistake, as such can be purchased. There should not be any remission of the hut tax, or help of any kind, except, of course, in very special cases. What we wish to avoid is that broadcast assistance which the Government has been so prone to give in the past.[50]

The authorities shared these views. When the Administrator, Sir William Milton, reported the danger of famine in April 1903, the Directors of the British South Africa Company warned him to 'consider most carefully the measure to be taken in order to both minimize expenses and to avoid pauperising any section of the population, whether white or black. It is thought that, as far as possible, relief should be given only in return for work, and that while there is time and where great difficulty of transport exists the population.....transfer themselves from the outlying districts to more accessible centres where food could be provided more cheaply and work can be given.'[51] Milton responded instantly. 'Natives have been informed', he cabled the next day, 'they will have to purchase food and fetch it themselves from distributing centres on the railway'.[52] When the Native Commissioner in Lomagundi suggested sending relief food to the Zambezi valley by mule wagon, Milton forbade it:

> It is perfectly impossible to feed whole tribes in such a locality by mule wagon. The mule feed for double journey will take 2,000 lbs off the load. The only feasible course is to move the people to some accessible spot and insist upon the men going to work. At the Ayreshire (mine) in this very district they are in want of 400 boys.[53]

The government's famine policy of 1903 therefore rested on two principles. One, already orthodox policy in India and South Africa, was to rely wherever possible on private trade. 'No natives have been assisted with grain as I did not consider it necessary', the Native Commissioner reported from Hartley. 'Money appears to be plentiful, and, where food was required, natives were able to purchase from their more prosperous neighbours and from local traders.'[54] Generally, however, European traders — and almost all licensed traders were Europeans — played little part in relieving this famine, partly perhaps because they were accustomed to buy grain from Africans and sell it to Europeans, partly because their selling prices were higher than those which Africans charged one another. Few price statistics survive from 1903, but in July people from the Zambezi valley could buy grain from African producers further south for between 15s. and 17s. 6d.a bag, whereas in May the average price of grain delivered to European mine-owners was 30s.a bag and was not expected to fall in the immediate future.[55] The problem was that European traders bore heavy transport costs as soon as they moved away from the railways, especially during drought when draught-animals were vulnerable and inefficient. Transport costs also deterred Africans from buying government grain at 'cost' price. As the Native Commissioner in Salisbury explained, 'They state that they are able to procure food from other sources at a lower rate'.[56] Only in the most extreme scarcity, as in Lomagundi District during November, would people undertake to perform labour in the future in return for an immediate supply of seed-grain.

The second principle of famine policy was that men should earn money to buy food by migrating to wage employment, the demand for labour being such at this time that there was no suggestion of opening the public works which were the normal means of relieving famine in the labour-surplus societies of India. In February 1903, for example, the Native Commissioner in Umtali announced that he would assist only the families of men who went out to work. And many men did seek work, even at the 10s.a month often paid to farmworkers or amid the appalling conditions of contemporary gold mines. 'Many young Natives have applied to me for work', Meredith reported from Melsetter in April, 'and others have applied for passes to seek work at the (Witwatersrand?) mines. The fact is that starvation and the approaching Hut tax collection period are making work a necessity and all the young men will have to go to work this year.'[57] In June a European newspaper noted that the famine had swollen the supply of mine labour. This was to be its normal effect in Belingwe District.[58]

Yet there were many complaints of refusal to accept employment, especially in Mashonaland. Nor was there any flight to the towns in 1903, as in Matabeleland in 1896. Rather, most people chose to stay at home and see the famine through. In some prosperous districts such as Makoni they may have been anxious to preserve their status as independent peasants,[59] but the response was most common in remote areas like the Zambezi valley. There the people gave another explanation, at least as recorded by officials. 'Where the shortage was greatest, little or no labour was forthcoming', the Chief Native Commissioner in Mashonaland reported:

> This was contrary to expectations, as it was thought that all able-bodied men would have taken the advice given to go out to work in order to leave the small quantity of grain on hand for their women and children. They, however, looked at it from a different point of view, and considered it necessary to remain at home and dig roots, hunt, fish, and gather wild fruit for their families.[60]

A Chief from the Zambezi valley gave a more chauvinistic version: 'In cases of starvation the men were the mainstay of the family as they did most of the hunting for roots, tortoises, and game, and that they could not possibly leave their women, because if they did so the women would most assuredly refuse to live with them as husbands on their return and they would thus lose their wives.' The same explanation was given in Hartley District on the highveld.[61] Moreover, as perceptive officials realized, where no grain was available in their home areas for families to buy with cash, it would have been irresponsible for men to undertake migrant labour.[62]

These responses emphasized the fact that famine survival in 1903 owed little to government aid or the European economy. This was a traditional famine met chiefly by traditional means, especially by exploiting wild produce. So long as that was available, men would stay at home, eat forest products, and preserve their families. So strong was this inherited pattern of behaviour that many groups had no notion that the government had any role in famine. Although his Melsetter District suffered severely, Meredith did not receive a single request for grain.[63] His colleague in Lomagundi recorded:

> The Chief Nomotombo (from the Zambezi valley) visited me during the month for the purpose of representing the bad condition they were in; but in answer to my question whether he was seeking Government assistance he replied that he had only come down to state that they were without food and that their crops had failed.
> I should expect them to ask for a remission of this year's Hut Tax, but I have not yet heard anything to that effect.[64]

Moreover, even if those worst affected by famine had looked to the government for aid, they would have received little, for this was a famine in remote areas where not even the government's writ yet ran, much less its roads. When Meredith planned to store grain for the people of Melsetter, he suggested that it should be deposited on the railway at Umtali, 150 laborious kilometres from his office and 200 from his more remote subjects — who were to *fetch* it.[65] When Fynn, in North Mazoe, was asked during October 1903 'why the Government were not issuing food to the natives in this District', he replied ' that owing to scarcity of transport, it would be difficult to ride sufficient grain from Salisbury even for a small proportion of the starving people'.[66] A month later he met some requests for seed, 'without stinting the horses', but he had to refuse requests for food because 'the limited supply of meal and grain in the Police Store will not allow of any issue to Natives. This is deplorable, as several Natives have died of starvation.'[67] On receiving this report a fortnight later, the authorities in Salisbury sent him a hundred bags of grain to issue at the cost price of 30s. a bag. It arrived after eleven days. At famine rations of one pound per person per day, this would have fed each person in his district for two days. It was all he received.

The government could do little to relieve the famine of 1903 in the most afflicted areas. Men had to rely instead on the means of survival which their ancestors had learned over the centuries. But the government could make things worse. At the height of the famine in 1903 the British South Africa Company decided to quadruple the hut tax to £2 a year, although the Colonial Office reduced this to £1. Native Commissioners spread the news in hungry villages. Arthur Shearly Cripps, who had seen men starve, wrote 'Black and White':

> Sing not 'Alas' for a starving land,
> For a tax to pay with an empty hand!
> To slave in a mine may be evil cheer —
> But the end of a life it is always near!
>
> Save an 'Alas' for the Strong and Free
> That were curst with the Weak man's company!
> They robbed as lightly as drew their breath —
> My God! Are they dead with the *second* death?[68]

41

# CHAPTER 5

## The Great Drought of 1912

The three years before the First World War[1] were a time of drought throughout the savanna regions of Africa, as also in India. In West Africa the worst famine since the mid-eighteenth century killed tens or hundreds of thousands. Drought extended eastwards to Ethiopia, stretched southwards through the arid lands of East Africa to the Cape, and curled back northwards to embrace Angola.[2]

In Southern Rhodesia, similarly, the drought was general and marked the lowest point of the rainfall decline which had begun during the 1880s. Its effects, however, were felt at different times in different regions. In Mashonaland an acute crisis followed the failure of the 1911/12 rains, which in Salisbury were only 68 per cent of the average — the lowest figure since the famine of 1903. There, however, the next season saw recovery, as also on the highveld of Matabeleland. In southern Matabeleland, by contrast, the crisis was prolonged; Hope Fountain, south of Bulawayo, received only 44, 67 and 73 per cent of average rainfall in the three years 1911/12, 1912/13, and 1913/14. The crisis was also prolonged in the Zambezi valley. Everywhere, however, this was a very great drought, which threatened — but did not in fact cause — a level of mortality which oral traditions compared to the time of the 'Swazi' invasion:

> The Natives are suffering from a famine, the like of which has not been experienced within human recollection. The old men say that the great famine that took place during the last years Zonkendaba — the Swazi Chief was travelling up the Sabi River, and which is known as the Gore Shangwa, is only the equal if not less than the present one. Now, as then, had there not been white people in the country to relieve their distress, the country would have been scattered with the bleached skulls of the hunger stricken people.[3]

This was recorded at Chibi, on the edge of the southern lowveld, and it was there — first in southern Mashonaland and its peripheries in 1912, then in southern Matabeleland in 1914 — that the famine was most severe.

The Mashonaland highveld, by contrast, escaped anything worse than scarcity, as in 1903. There was famine in the Dande in the extreme northeast and also in the lowveld areas of Mtoko District, where the government had to sell grain at cost price,[4] but the mediocre crops on the plateau carried the people through until excellent rains fell at the end of 1912. The highveld survived because it had enjoyed several years of prosperity and possessed sufficient reserves in grain, stock and cash. The government reckoned that between 1909 and 1912 Africans withdrew £735,000 from circulation and hoarded it.[5] Shona agriculture was especially flourishing, for Europeans had created a market which their own farms could only slowly satisfy. Many Shona had adopted more productive American maize seed. A few were using ploughs to produce rich crops from the heavier soils, occasionally hiring labour.[6] Herds were recovering from rinderpest. Wages in European employment, although low, were probably higher in real terms than at any time before the 1950s.[7] Admittedly, this relative prosperity was threatened. Serious European farming had begun and rents in cash or labour were regularly demanded from Africans living on White-owned property. But except in Inyanga and Umtali Districts, where most land was alienated, Shona generally lived in Reserves whose growing populations were not yet pressing on the available land. When Mashonaland's Chief Native Commissioner reported in 1907 that 'the majority of the natives of this Province are exceedingly well off'[8] he was certainly exaggerating, but he caught the mood of the highveld.

It was otherwise in the south. Nine years earlier, Fort Victoria District and the regions to its east and south had been the Mecca for grain traders, but by 1912 the area was deeply depressed. Railway construction had made it a backwater. The opening of a line from Gwelo to Selukwe in 1903 had enabled the mines to draw their grain from the highveld of central Mashonaland rather than the south.[9] There, so Professor Phimister has written, 'Peasants were no longer producing grain in any significant quantities for the market, the price having dropped too low. In fact, many were purchasing grain from Europeans with the profits they had won from the sale of livestock.'[10] In 1911 Fort Victoria District imported grain for the first time.[11] 'The greatest need of the place', a newspaper complained in 1912, 'is a railway to bring in supplies of food'.[12] In Fort Victoria District this decline was worsened by European settlement, which increased the proportion of Africans living in Native Reserves from 10 per cent in 1903 to nearly 50 per cent in 1912.[13] But the famine was to be even worse in the Chibi, Ndanga, and southern Melsetter districts where little land alienation had occurred. The famine of 1912 centred in the areas *least* affected by colonial change.

All these southern districts were already short of food at the beginning of 1912, for it took more than a single harvest failure to cause famine. 'The Natives', so Native Commissioner Bazeley wrote from Ndanga in January, 'are scattering in every direction in search of food', convinced that the coming harvest would fail.[14] February proved them right. The southern half of Ndanga District received almost no rain and its people were without food. In southern Chibi wild fruits and milk, supplemented by relief grain, were expected to last for only another two months. Further east, in the Sabi valley, the rainfall was the worst on record. 'Crops are a total failure in the Sabi Valley and other low lying parts and natives are already in some distress', the Native Commissioner reported from Melsetter in March:

> ....I estimate that the yield of grain on the high veldt will be less than half what is usual and this combined with the total failure of crops in other parts makes the position very critical. A large proportion of the native population will shortly be without food and forced to subsist on a precarious diet of wild fruits, grass seeds and roots. I am afraid the mortality will be heavy unless some arrangements are made to render assistance.[15]

Faced with crisis, Native Commissioners relied initially on the remedies employed during the famine of 1903. The first was to persuade men to leave their homes and seek employment with Europeans, both to relieve pressure on local food supplies and to earn cash with which to buy grain for their families. As in 1903, however, Africans responded in contrasting ways to this pressure. In Matabeleland and some higher regions of Mashonaland, food shortage swelled the labour supply. In Mtoko District, for example, 63 per cent of able-bodied men worked for an average of five and a half months.[16] In the southern lowveld, however, forest products offered an alternative source of food and men responded quite differently. 'I have tried to impress upon the Headmen the necessity of able bodied men going out to work to lessen the mouths to feed at each kraal, but they are very apathetic', an official wrote in March 1912 of Nyashano's drought-stricken chiefdom between the Devure and the Sabi. 'There is no doubt that the men do not like leaving their women when there is a shortage of food and it is hard to blame them.'[17] Officials therefore turned to the second remedy employed during 1903: to rely on trade. Hungry Africans were indeed already trading among themselves. 'Their method', Bazeley reported, 'was to take their bulls to a kraal where good crops had been reaped and there to kill them and barter the meat for grain'. He reckoned that 2 000 or 3 000 beasts were slaughtered in Ndanga District during the first six months of 1912.[18] But what officials meant by trade was reliance on European traders to transport grain into famine areas and exchange it for African cash or cattle. Such traders had done little to relieve the famine of 1903, but since then their numbers and their share of African trade had grown, their links with South Africa had strengthened, and they had gained access to supplies of the grain which hungry Africans needed, for since 1903 European farming in Southern Rhodesia had become a serious enterprise. In 1904 only

301 White farms had been occupied; in 1914 the number would be 2 042.[19] Europeans had grown 393 166 bags of maize in 1911 and had exported 23 378.[20] The traders, therefore, had something to sell, and they also had something to buy: cattle, African breeding stock to build up European herds.

During April 1912, therefore, Bazeley called in private traders to meet the threatening famine in southern Ndanga, but only to discover the hazards of this strategy:

> In those parts where the crops are a failure a serious famine already exists and thousands are starving though I cannot learn that there have yet been any deaths in consequence. Arrangements have been made with certain farmers and traders to ride a small amount of grain to worst parts which can be reached.... One farmer of the Victoria District has offered to supply 500 bags of mealies at 35/- to £2 a bag and probably those natives who have cattle will buy. The Europeans of the district have about 200 bags or rupoko, munga and mealies between them and are asking high prices. Unfortunately a large proportion of the starving natives have no cattle or money and will be unable to buy.... I calculate that about 10,000 natives have no food and will have to be fed somehow for the next nine months.[21]

The point of relying on private trade was to develop a commercial system which could prevent famine by moving food quickly to areas of shortage and high prices. The difficulty was that the high prices needed to attract traders were beyond the means of the poor, who were most of the hungry. And prices were indeed high. During 1911 maize had sold in the main centres at less than 9s. a bag, but in December 1911 and January 1912 the expectation of drought had suddenly increased the price to 20s. or more.[22] These prices attracted grain from the vastly greater supplies in South Africa, which ultimately governed prices in Salisbury and Bulawayo.[23] In Salisbury, the minimum wholesale price of a bag (203 lb.) of white maize began the year 1912 at 20s., fell to 15s. between May and September, and then rose to 24s. early in 1913.[24] Bulawayo prices began the year at 20s. a bag, fell to 18s. during the winter, and rose to over 25s. at the end of the year.[25] Sorghum usually cost about the same and finger millet about 5s. more per bag. The fluctuations during 1912 were quite small: only about 25 per cent on each side of the average price. But the contrast with 1911 was great, and prices in rural areas varied enormously with the season and transport costs. Early in 1912, for example, Shona growers in remote Mtoko sold finger millet for 5s. a bag, whereas the ruling price for maize in Makoni District (on the railway line) was between 15s. and 20s. At the end of the year, finger millet fetched 45s. a bag in Mtoko, the same as the price for maize in Fort Victoria and rather less than the 50s. demanded in Gutu.[26] In Ndanga District government sold grain in December 1912 at a cost price of 42s. a bag, as against the normal local price of about 5s.[27] Fluctuations were smaller — only twofold or threefold — in less remote districts, but often they were exaggerated by being calculated in terms of cattle, whose prices tended to fall as grain prices rose. In Gutu District, for example, men bought cattle from less fortunate neighbours early in 1912 for five or even six bags of grain per beast but were said to be reselling them a year later for two or sometimes only one bag.[28] The European traders who supplied Fort Victoria District during 1912 bought some 2 000 cattle, often giving only one bag of grain for a cow or heifer.[29] To prevent cattle prices collapsing was a crucial difficulty with the free enterprise strategy of famine relief.

High cost was one drawback to private trade. The other was that animal transport made it practicable only within restricted areas. 'Natives in the upper portion of the district whose crops have failed are able to buy from European traders', it was reported from Chibi in April 1912, 'but those further to the south are unable to do so, owing to the limited amount of grain held by the traders and their selling out to the people of the upper part'.[30] The six traders then operating in Chibi District could supply only 500-600 bags a month. The government had supplied some food at cost price since the beginning of the year and tried to direct this to areas not reached by traders, but by May the government agents were finding that many people had no reserves with which to buy. To meet this difficulty, the Administrator, Sir William Milton, ordered on 21 May that food might be issued on credit to the able-bodied in proportion to the length of time for which they engaged to work, although free issues might be made only to the incapacitated.[31] The intention was that the government should feed the families of men who left home to earn cash with which they would subsequently pay for the food. In Ndanga, however, Bazeley found total hostility to this scheme:

> The natives at present refuse absolutely to accept any advance of grain or meal either from private individuals or from the Government. I have tried very hard to learn their reasons for this attitude; but, as is usual with natives, they will not give me the true one. Probably the main reason is a rooted dislike on general grounds to loans from either the Government or from any European. Another is that they hope to be able to raise some food from neighbouring natives. I hear too that they are declaring that as they have paid tax for so many years to the Government they are entitled to free food in their time of need; but this has not been directly stated to me by any of those concerned.[32]

The government's fear of 'pauperization' clashed with African expecta-

46

tions of reciprocity. Many may have realized that famine relief on credit — *mucheneko,* as Shona called it[33] — was an onerous burden, for it came at famine prices but had to be repaid from normal wages. 'In 1903', a Native Commissioner reported, '... they found they had to work so long to pay off the advance, that any similar experience is regarded with distinct aversion'.[34]

Yet the crisis was deepening. In May 1912 Bazeley reckoned that several thousand people in Ndanga District 'have neither food nor the means wherewith to purchase it'. His assistant in Bikita, C.S. Blackwell, estimated 'that at least 7600 people are starving' and demanded a major relief operation.[35] The authorities in Salisbury sent a prominent Native Commissioner, C.L. Carbutt, to investigate conditions in the south. Officials there told him that 29 000 people would need assistance in Chibi District and 10 000 in Ndanga, but Carbutt thought the latter figure a serious underestimate. European traders were supplying the upper parts of Chibi District, but they had too little grain to feed the lowveld and the distances were prohibitive. People in Chibi still had stock and could barter it for grain. In Ndanga, too, they had stock, but private trade was less effective, a handful of deaths had occurred, 'and many people are in too emaciated a condition to go in search of food'. Carbutt suggested that since men refused to leave this region to seek work, local road-building should be started.[36] Little came of this constructive suggestion, however, and it may already have been too late, for famine relief works must precede serious emaciation.

Carbutt found, as local officials already knew, that the problem was to transport enough food to the distant areas where famine was worst. As Native Commissioner Forrestall in Chibi put it, 'Most of the natives have either the cattle or the money, but cannot get the grain'.[37] In July, therefore, the Native Department intervened to improve supplies. Forrestall opened a government post at which people could exchange stock for food. Blackwell patrolled the Bikita lowveld, found several European traders, and concluded that 'reports of starvation had been exaggerated'. 'The only present anxiety I have is for the poorer class of natives, who have nothing to give in exchange for grain', he added. 'I have informed headmen that if these people and their families come and stay near this station, they will receive free rations every day. I consider this course will discourage any but bona-fide applicants, and trust the Government will endorse my action.'[38] Nobody took advantage of this offer until November. Meanwhile Bazeley toured his enormous Ndanga District with the aim of opening transport routes and establishing a relief system. He first visited the western border, improved the terrible wagon road from Fort Victoria, arranged for private traders to bring in grain, and investigated cases of starvation. He found 230 indigent, starving families in a population of 5 716 and issued free food to '75 families who were emaciated with hunger and which had neither food nor property nor supporters'.[39] Then he turned southwards to the Nyajena Reserve and found the famine worse but not yet extreme; he listed 95 starving families among a population of 3 608 who still possessed 1 537 cattle and had 673 bags of grain in their bins.[40] Finally Bazeley reached the area between the Mutirikwi and Tokwe rivers, and found a nightmare:

> Being far away from the grain regions the natives had not been able to get any supplies. The majority were living entirely on the fruits of the 'Shuma' tree and on vermin and roots. These swell the stomach but do not nourish the limbs. Many of the older men and the women and children were in a pitiable condition of emaciation. I only heard of five deaths from starvation all of them old men and women. At one kraal a woman was found lying dead of starvation all the rest of the kraal having fled into the veldt. Two or three natives seemed on the point of death but were revived with broth.[41]

Bazeley listed 135 starving families among a population of 2 108 who possessed 696 cattle but only 100 bags of grain between them. 'In order to stave off immediate starvation',[42] he authorized the most needy to collect 144 bags of grain from a neighbouring European rancher named Robinson. 'All who had property of any kind were informed that they might purchase grain at Mr Robinson's either for cash or with breeding cattle. Adult male natives who were starving were told to go out to work.'[43] Bazeley also arranged for the construction of a wagon road through the hills to open up the south of his district, to be built by local labour in return for food.

In Salisbury, meanwhile, Sir William Milton was pondering famine strategy. Southern Rhodesia had no famine code on the Indian model. Nor, it appears, had South Africa, where Milton had previously worked, but it had a tradition of expecting starving Africans to work, encouraging private trade, giving some help with transport, and confining direct relief to the incapacitated.[44] This tradition rested ultimately on the principles of nineteenth-century political economy, or what a Victorian administrator grimly called 'the operation of natural causes'.[45] Southern Rhodesian officials had drawn on these principles when responding to the famine of 1903. Now, with one eye always on the settler community, Milton defined a policy. In May he authorized relief to the incapacitated but ordered that the able-bodied should receive food only on credit in return for an engagement to work. In August, as the incapacitated multiplied and reliance on private trade and migrant labour faced collapse, Milton made *mucheneko* the centrepiece of his policy:

> I consider that no free issues should be made, but that grain should be advanced on condition of repayment after a given period, where natives have not cash or stock to pay at once. Chiefs and Headmen should be held responsible for repayment.
>
> If free issues are once given there is no knowing where it will stop, and the liability of natives who are possessed of means or can earn them to support those who are ordinarily dependent on them must be insisted on. Otherwise we shall have to provide for all older members of families and no effort on the part of the ablebodied men can be looked for.[46]

Disturbed by this ruthlessness, Chief Native Commissioner Taylor of Matabeleland — who had seen men starve in 1896 — urged that kraal heads rather than Chiefs should be held responsible and that 'there must always be a few instances of isolated paupers, who are such even in good times and are then dependent on the generosity of other natives, but who will probably not get this assistance in hard times, and these few cases will require assistance from the Government'. Milton grudgingly conceded. 'My object', he noted, 'is not simply to save expense, but to avoid pauperisation as far as possible'.[47] Native Commissioners were, therefore, instructed that no free issues of food must be made, but only advances on condition of repayment, if necessary by kraal heads, with the rider that 'Native Commissioners will of course understand that real distress must be relieved'.[48]

At the same time Milton appointed Major J.S. Masterman, the Ordnance Officer of the British South Africa Police, to take charge of relief. Given that the Police and Native Commissioners had been at odds for nearly twenty years, this was a drastic step, but Masterman immediately infused urgency. His task, he explained on 17 August, was to induce private traders to supply grain and exchange it for cattle at reasonable rates, supplying it himself only where traders declined. Early in September he toured the famine area in Ndanga and Bikita and returned optimistic. 'I believe we are in touch with the whole of the situation now', he wrote, 'and although the position is no doubt serious, do not think there is any cause for alarm, as so many agencies are at work to provide grain'.[49] Private traders were in place to supply Chibi and the lowveld areas of Melsetter. Masterman hoped they might even provide for southern Ndanga now that a road existed, but in the meantime Bazeley — informed that his previous free issues were contrary to instructions — had turned to supplying grain as a loan against deferred payment and reported 'a remarkable change of attitude as regards these loans'.[50]

It was during October 1912 that the new strategy collapsed. In Bikita, for example, helpless people simply ignored the principles of political economy:

> I shall be glad to know what is to be done with old men and women, cripples, blind natives, who have no relatives willing to look after them or whose relatives are finding it too big a struggle to feed their own families without having to look after their unfortunate relations. These people refused to take a loan and in any case would be unable to repay.[51]

Masterman warned Milton of the danger:

> I refer to instructions free issues. I now fear that interpretation of same will result in some cases of destitution being unrelieved and preventable mortality ensue. May I please be allowed to authorise officials in affected areas in this circle to relieve absolute cases of distress. I am anxious that we should minimise the possibility of deaths from starvation and also be able to rebut any charges of callousness which might be levied against us... Kraal heads Chibi refuse to accept responsibility for repayment.[52]

'No real case of destitution should go unrelieved', Milton noted briefly, and would go no further.[53] Meanwhile the second plank of his policy was cracking. Private transport was disappearing from the wagon-routes because famine was spreading from men to animals. 'Owners of waggons refuse to ride owing to lack of grass', Bazeley reported from Ndanga.[54] No transport rider was willing to use the new road to the south, where reports of deaths were increasing. Those still operating 'get rid of everything before they get down (to the south), though the natives above are really in no real danger of starving'. 'Private enterprise is not coping with the situation to the extent that we expected it would', Masterman complained. '....Unless we get plenty of rain within the next fortnight I fear a complete breakdown of what little ox transport is left. So far as our own transport is concerned I shall start feeding with mealies to keep them going.'[55] And still the famine spread. 'The shortage in the District appears to have entered on a new phase', Bazeley reported early in November. 'It has extended all over the District.... The Natives round this Station are now clamouring for grain to be sold or loaned to them, though they had not been previously regarded as starving. I have sold 113 bags in the past month and could have disposed of at least three times that amount if I had had it.'[56] Further to the east a new famine area emerged at the end of October in the Sabi valley, where officials reported severe want, especially among refugees from Mozambique, several of whom had died of starvation.[57] Private trade in this region had collapsed and the agent of the only European still holding stocks was selling at £4 per bag, the highest price recorded anywhere during the famine but later said to have been an error. 'There will be a large percentage of deaths among the older people as soon as the rains set in unless a more substantial form of food is available for them', it was reported.[58] Masterman was desperate. 'No difficulty about grain it is transport that presents trouble', he cabled before setting off to inspect.[59]

Early in November Masterman reached Melsetter from railhead at Umtali by motor car — the only use of these novel vehicles during this famine. The road was atrocious. Ox-transport was prohibited for fear of introducing East Coast Fever into settler herds in Melsetter. The only vehicles available were wagons drawn by donkeys or mules, whose charges — 2s. per ton-mile — raised the price of grain in the Sabi valley to 50s. a bag. Masterman bought or hired all the available transport and set up a distribution system manned by his policemen.[60] One post reported itself 'almost in a state of siege. Numbers of natives are camped in the vicinity and will not go away, being afraid of missing the waggons as they arrive.'[61] This was now the pattern throughout the southern lowveld. 'The Natives are clamouring for grain from the whole district', Bazeley reported from Ndanga. '....The private traders have now failed altogether. They must now be left out of the reckoning. All now depends on the amount of transport obtainable by the Ordnance Officer.'[62] Everywhere hungry people were still relying more on wild produce than on the small quantities of grain which the authorities could provide. In the three months to 28 November Masterman's organization supplied only 7 626 bags of grain to all the needy districts in the colony,[63] or enough to feed nearly 50 000 people for one month at famine rations. Meanwhile the European press, having discovered that famine existed, printed statements 'urging upon the Government the necessity of withholding further supplies of grain and thereby forcing the native to come forward into the labour market instead of awaiting at his kraal the ministrations of a beneficent Government'.[64] Milton tried to refute these criticisms before departing at the end of November for two months leave at the Cape. His last report noted that the drought was breaking.[65]

For Masterman and his transport riders that was a mixed blessing. Fresh wild produce would soon be available, crops might be close to harvest within three or four months, and there was grass and water for draught animals. But to drag grain-laden wagons through the mud of a rainy season was an appalling task. During December the route from Umtali became almost impassable, 'very few of the donkey wagons engaged dared face the road after one trip',[66] and only 290 bags reached Melsetter. Ferocious opposition from local settlers stopped Masterman using oxen. Further west the road from Umvuma to Fort Victoria had to be abandoned and there was acute shortage in the south of Fort Victoria District. Chibi ran out of supplies and even the imperturbable Forrestall — an American and former sailor — was appalled:

> I disposed of 100 bags at Shindi's Kraal on the Sunday before Christmas, and I estimated at the same time that there was some £200 in cash unspent, and over 100 head of cattle driven away by their disappointed owners. Some refused to leave unless something was given them. This was done as far as possible in the shape of a couple of handsfull. In the distribution grain is made to go as far as possible, no person being allowed to buy more than a few shillings' worth, and cattle were bought on the system of paying one bag and owing one: it of course trebles the work, but that is no matter so that as many as possible can be helped. The heart of an official must indeed be of stone if he stays amongst his starving Natives with nothing to give them.[67]

In Chibi, as in Melsetter, a few more deaths from starvation were added to the count. Yet the worst problem was still in Ndanga, where only 645 bags were distributed during December, as against the 2 000 which Bazeley thought a minimum. 'When any waggon arrives', he reported, 'the official in charge of the distribution is immediately surrounded by crowds of Natives with money or cattle sufficient to buy far more than is delivered.'[68] Many had planted their seed before the rains, not only to seek an early crop but to remove the temptation to eat it. In Bikita, Blackwell's invitation to the incapacitated to take refuge near his headquarters had attracted a host of destitute people dependent on relief rations. He issued free food to 213 adults and 166 dependents during the famine. Of the adults, 157 were women (85 of them with children), 42 old men, 3 blind, and 5 cripples.[69] Their condition was especially acute early in February 1913, but rain then fell and Blackwell finally closed his relief operations on 26 April. He had issued grain worth £3 670, of which £85 was issued free and £1 435 on credit. Three years later Ndanga and Bikita still had large unpaid debts for food issued on credit during this famine and it had become part of folklore that Bazeley and Blackwell had distributed relief recklessly, although their superiors hotly denied it.[70]

Elsewhere in southern Mashonaland relief operations also ended during February 1913. Twenty people were reported to have starved to death during March in the Sabi valley, but even there wild produce was plentiful and the people could generally survive by customary means.[71] Ndanga also reported occasional deaths at that time but little demand for government grain, an observation echoed in Chibi and Fort Victoria. Most remarkably, there had been no epidemic disease. The only epidemics of 1912 were minor smallpox outbreaks in several northern districts, acute influenza in the Insiza District of Matabeleland, a severe measles epidemic which killed great numbers of children in Sebungwe District near the Zambezi, and an increase in scurvy among mine workers.[72] Yet southern Mashonaland was desperately impoverished. 'Many were far too poor in condition to make gardens', Forrestall reported of his worst-affected area, '.... as each ear ripens it is taken for food. There will be no general harvest and no grain will go into the bins.'[73] Ndanga took years to recover.

While the rains of early 1913 ended famine in southern Mashonaland, other regions were less fortunate. The people of the Zambezi valley suffered longest. In May 1912 'something like starvation' existed there.[74] Three months later a patrolling Native Commissioner found women miles from home scouring the bush for wild fruit. Crops from riverside gardens temporarily relieved the shortage, but it returned in November and the government could do little to help people so isolated by distance and tsetse-infested bush. In December the scarcity of food caused a strike at Wankie Colliery.[75] The rains of early 1913 were exceptionally erratic and further scarcity ensued. The pattern was repeated in 1914, when the Valley Tonga people on the northern bank began to take refuge on the neighbouring plateau. Late in 1914 and early in 1915, when the rest of Southern Rhodesia enjoyed exceptionally heavy rains, floods destroyed the crops in the valley. Famine was reported somewhere in the area every year between 1915 and 1918. It was perhaps the longest, if not the most intense, period of hunger in local memory.[76]

Yet Tonga were accustomed to famine. More significant for the future were events between 1912 and 1915 in Matabeleland. Since the dearth of the early 1860s, this region had been remarkably free of famine, save in the exceptional circumstances of 1896. Most of the records of its harvest failure in 1903 have disappeared, but it appears to have done little damage.[77] In 1912, however, the region suffered almost universal food shortage as a result of a drought-stricken harvest which Native Commissioner Thomas — who had been born there in 1865 — described as 'the worst I have ever known in this country'.[78] Grain had been scarce even when 1912 began. The first area of serious shortage was Belingwe, bordering Chibi in the extreme east of Matabeleland, where government supplies were needed in February 1912 and continued to be necessary throughout the year to supplement the grain offered by private traders. The Native Commissioner estimated that his district imported 30 000 bags during 1912.[79] The other centre of dearth was Thomas's district of Bulalima-Mangwe in the extreme south-west, bordering famine-stricken Bechuanaland and the Kalahari. Here there was 'great distress' at the Empandeni and Embakwe missions in April 1912. Six months later,

'Practically the bulk of Empandeni's population (over 2 000) have to be provided with food'.[80] In October the government began to sell grain in Gwanda District, in the lowveld south-east of Bulawayo. A month later Masterman was supplying all these districts and also Filabusi and Nyamandhlovu. Grain prices rose to 40s. a bag, but most purchasers could offer cattle, for between 1901 and 1911 African herds in Matabeleland had increased (according to dubious figures) from 13 000 to 117 000.[81] In Gwanda, famed for the quality of its cattle, prices fell by 30 per cent during 1912, but heifers still averaged about £5, while the best oxen and cows with calves fetched up to £10.[82] Unlike the southern Shona, moreover, Ndebele did not refuse labour migration during famine. 'Every available working male has this year been out to work for at least 8 months of the year.... due purely and solely to the poor harvest reaped', the Native Commissioner in Bubi reported.[83] Altogether the authorities estimated that Matabeleland bought some 75 000 bags of grain during the year, paying 15 000 cattle and £30 000 in cash.[84]

The most difficult question about Matabeleland's shortage is whether it owed anything to the effects of land alienation, especially to the gradual drift from European estates, which accommodated 84 000 Africans in 1908 and 61 256 in 1912, to the lower-lying Native Reserves, the population of which rose in that period from 78 000 to 91 103.[85] The overall scarcity of land was still slight, although growing. 'The native reserves are capable of carrying a far larger population than they do at present', the Chief Native Commissioner mused in 1912, 'but the natives' holdings in stock are increasing at a very rapid rate, so that it is doubtful whether in a few years their capacity will not be limited for this purpose.'[86] On the other hand, the concentration of scarcity in lowveld pastoral districts like Gwanda and Bulalima-Mangwe in 1912 might suggest that some pressure on grazing was already emerging, as might the numerous references to stock deaths. Yet these borderlands of the Kalahari would have been vulnerable in any drought so severe as that of 1912. What is clear is that the pattern of famine which later became predominant — famine centred in the lowveld of Matabeleland — first appeared at this time.

Ironically, although Bulawayo had much less rain in 1912/13 and 1913/14 than in 1911/12, the drought on the highveld of Matabeleland was largely broken in February 1913. In the south-western lowveld, however, only moderate rain fell at that time and scarcity continued almost without interruption until the end of 1914. In April 1913 the Jesuits at Empandeni recorded that only 460 mm of rain had fallen during the previous 26 months.[87] Several families had already left. The men had gone to work, sending home what they could, but the old, the young, and the women left behind displayed 'the expression of sullen despair'.[88] Two months later the Fathers were feeding several dozens of them; at least one woman had starved to death. The rains failed again in 1913/14, only 240 mm falling at Empandeni.[89] More families abandoned the area, but the starving crowds grew larger. Late in 1914 the missionaries reported that rain had fallen on slightly more than 30 days during the previous three years.[90] Almost immediately it came in torrents — nearly 900 mm by February 1915. 'Hope is reviving in the hearts of our poor natives', the Fathers rejoiced.[91] They reckoned that the drought had claimed fifty lives in the area.[92]

The contrast between the one-season food shortage on the highveld, the severe but relatively brief famine in southern Mashonaland, and the long-drawn agonies of the Kalahari fringes and the Zambezi valley reveals most clearly the differential effects of drought in Southern Rhodesia's varied environments. The other main feature of this famine is that it was the first in which the colonial government made a significant contribution to relief. This was mainly an old-style famine: it was due to severe drought, was worst in peripherial areas with little European presence, and was met chiefly by ancient techniques of storage, foraging, and barter. Yet the famine did display more transitional elements than that of 1903. In particular, men relied more heavily than before on the European economy. They sought employment and they bartered cattle to European traders in return for grain. They also relied on official relief, although to a lesser extent — only perhaps 4 000 of the 20 000 bags of grain distributed in Chibi District were supplied by the government, while the 75 000 bags thought to have been sold in Matabeleland might be compared with the 9 000 which Masterman's organization had supplied to all parts of the colony by the end of November.[93]

One bag of grain might keep one adult alive for 200 days. When Masterman received the British South Africa Company's 'high appreciation of the energy and ability displayed by him',[94] therefore, it could be less for the total quantity he had distributed than for the strategic points at which he had made it available and the immense difficulties of transport he had overcome. In all he had opened 24 distribution depots by the end of 1912 and had spent £19 000 on grain and nearly £15 000 on transport.[95] Together with the work of Bazeley and his colleagues, this operation may have prevented much mortality in southern Mashonaland during this exceptionally severe drought.

# CHAPTER 6

## The Ndanga Famine, 1916

On the surface, the famine of 1916 repeated that of 1912.[1] Once again drought created widespread scarcity which was least serious on the highveld and most intense at the peripheries, especially in the lower parts of the Ndanga and Bikita area of southern Mashonaland, where the severity of the famine and the fullness of the sources justify special treatment. Beneath the surface, however, were important shifts of emphasis. Although the famine of 1916 was caused by drought, its severity in particular localities, especially Ndanga, owed much to pre-existing poverty. Methods of survival suggest rather more dependence than hitherto on wage-labour, European trade, and government relief, a tendency encouraged by the expansion of European agriculture and by shifts in famine policy. Above all, few if any people died directly from famine in 1916. It marked a further stage in the transition from indigenous techniques of famine control to those of the twentieth century.

Following the great drought of 1912, Mashonaland experienced two years of good rainfall, while Matabeleland suffered continued drought, especially in the south. Then the climate showed its true unpredictability in 1914/15 by producing too much rain: Bulawayo received 901 mm, as against 396 in the previous year, and several areas suffered crop failure, especially in southern Mashonaland. In the summer of 1915/16, however, universal drought returned. Rainfall in Bulawayo was only 413 mm (68 per cent of average), in Salisbury 603 mm (73 per cent), in Fort Victoria 366 mm (57 per cent), and in Victoria Falls 378 mm (54 per cent) — the last two being the lowest figures since records began. Predictions of universal disaster filled the first months of 1916. Early in March the Chief Native Commissioner reported 'the severest drought experienced' and beggars appeared in the streets of Bulawayo.[2] A fortnight later, however, good rains fell just in time to save the harvest in central, northern, and eastern Mashonaland, so that although estimated African grain production per head was only 58 per cent of the previous season's,[3] the crops varied dramatically in different regions.

In Mrewa District in the north-east, for example, crops were good, prices high by local standards, and traders quick to buy everything offered. The same was true in the red-soil areas of Makoni District, where a generation of Shona peasants had created a prosperity which their Native Commissioner described in September 1916:

I came upon three different places where traders had stacked about 100 bags of grain they had bought for cash from the natives. In another part I met three wagons loaded with grain so bought and the owners informed me they were going back to fetch other loads. Another trader wrote notifying me he had bought 300 bags of grain and was then about to cart them away. I met in other places strings of native women carrying grain for sale — the price usually paid was 2/- a basket.

Very considerable numbers of cattle have been sold this year. The natives.... live mainly on Reserves, and customarily rely on the sale of cattle and grain for the payment of taxes, and for the purchase of any commodities.[4]

Two months later, by contrast, a local settler reported 'the famine-stricken appearance of many of the natives', perhaps because crops on lighter soils had failed. The harvest showed a similar unevenness in Lomagundi District.[5]

To the south and west of Salisbury, by contrast, 1916 was a year of scarcity. Even hitherto prosperous Chilimanzi experienced its worst year since the British occupation and needed famine relief for the first time, but the official in Fort Victoria who supervised the whole region regarded Chilimanzi as his least-affected district. He reckoned that food purchases cost his subjects at least £50 000 during the year.[6] Apart from Ndanga, which is considered later, the worst scarcity was in the Sabi and Lundi valleys.

Matabeleland, too, suffered serious shortage during 1916, but again it was uneven. The late rains during March saved the crops at drought-ridden Empandeni, for example, and everywhere they saved the pastures and the cattle, but Gwanda District reaped only one-tenth of a normal crop[7] and all the districts surrounding Bulawayo reported at least partial harvest failure.

As usual at this period, however, the famine was more severe on the northern peripheries of the colony. In Mount Darwin district the crops failed completely in the Dande, where in February district messengers 'had to travel at night and wear sandals to prevent the soles of their feet getting burnt by the sand'.[8] By April the people were living on the bush and in October messengers reported very severe starvation. There is no direct evidence of deaths in this rarely-visited region, but several men from the Mount Darwin District who took jobs on the Shamva Mine died 'owing to their extreme poor physique consequent on semi-starvation'.[9] Yet scarcely anyone from the Dande climbed the escarpment to obtain the grain which the government held available at Mount Darwin.

Further west, the Tonga of the Zambezi valley had not enjoyed a normal harvest since 1911. As their Native Commissioner wrote, 'What would be termed "want" by the Southern natives is a situation regarded by local tribes, especially the Batonka, as a more or less normal state of affairs'.[10] Distress was reported among them in January 1916 and, after some relief from riverside gardens in September, distress was reported again in December. Although the Native Commissioner held relief grain in readiness, tsetse fly prevented animal transport beyond his office and distances were such that 'natives coming in to buy would be no better off than they were before, as the greater part of what they bought would be consumed on the return journey'.[11] Even Tonga visiting the office took little advantage of the grain available. They exploited their extraordinary knowledge of wild produce. They hunted. They cultivated every patch of damp soil. 'On some stretches of the river, miles in length, were to be seen one continuous line of gardens', the Native Commissioner reported.[12] They bartered with the people of neighbouring plateaux or worked for them in return for food. Many travelled westwards to Wankie Colliery, often arriving emaciated but refusing either to work on the mine or to seek government relief. 'They prefer to beg for food, or earn a little by hawking firewood', a local official explained.[13] Even in starvation, it appears, the stateless Tonga maintained their independence.

Wankie was a major famine centre in 1916. So severe was the drought early in the year that not even the wild grasses yielded their customary famine foods. With only a 10 per cent harvest, the people survived for some months largely on roots and wild fruits, but in July relief food was needed. By October everyone was dependent on grain obtained from traders or the government. The Native Commissioner reported emaciation, disease — dysentery, chicken-pox, measles, whooping-cough, and cerebro-spinal meningitis — a lack of time and strength to cultivate new fields, and 'a general state of demoralization':

> Family ties are severed; women and children neglected; while young and able-bodied men go wandering about in the veldt in search of roots and other edibles, loath to be under restraining influence, such as regular employment. Immorality is on the increase, and I have good reason for believing that the womenfolk are frequently encouraged by the men to 'eat the bread of shame' and supply their homes with the earnings of immorality.
>
> So far 800 bags of grain have been issued departmentally to the Natives. I estimate 1200 bags to have been sold privately; further, for a considerable time past probably 1-200 bags per month of meal issued by the Colliery as rations to the employees are disposed of by them to their relatives, friends, and others.[14]

The Native Commissioner added, however, that rain had already fallen. It was only 10 November and it was raining almost everywhere in the colony. Although total precipitation in 1916/17 was mediocre, the fact that the early rains were generous almost certainly prevented the famine from causing the fatalities which otherwise clustered around the end of the year. 'Owing to the recent rains', the Chief Native Commissioner reported early in December, 'wild fruits have come up to such an extent that it has been decided that the continuance of famine relief after the end of this month will be unnecessary.'[15] The famine of 1916 was over.

That the appearance of wild produce was the signal to end official relief indicates how important the bush remained as a means of survival. It was mentioned chiefly, however, with regard to peripheral lowveld areas. Elsewhere these resources may have been less easily available to Africans who clustered in Reserves or enjoyed limited rights on White land. As a missionary wrote of the dearth of 1916 in Northern Rhodesia, 'Now a famine is more serious than in the olden days, when the people were fewer and the veldt richer in wild fruits'.[16] This may help to explain why lowveld peoples in particular resisted labour migration during famine. 'Their natural and ineradicable instinct', the Chief Native Commissioner reported, 'is to remain at home during times of famine and forage for their dependents'.[17] Elsewhere, however, famine conditions generally swelled the supply of labour, despite declining wages.[18]

A growing reliance on the White economy was most obvious in the greater role played in 1916 by European traders. As in previous famines, official policy was to rely upon them wherever possible. 'In those parts where the natives are short the headmen have asked me to request that grain be sent in at once', the Native Commissioner reported from Gutu in May 1916:

> I have therefore arranged with Messrs Meikle Bros., Levason, Burrows, and others to take grain to these parts. This having been satisfactorily arranged, there will be no need for the Government to send grain in, other than that which will be required to assist natives who cannot buy from traders. I still consider that at least 10,000 bags will be used, or even more, so there is scope for a lot of trading.[19]

The traders rarely needed encouragement. Nothing was more striking about this famine than the eagerness with which they took advantage of it. 'There are indications already', the Native Commissioner wrote from Charter in April, 'of speculators making efforts to secure trading sites and hawkers licences for the purpose of cornering all grain and sell to the natives later on at exhorbitant prices'.[20] Nor was this only a survival strategy for poor Whites. In 1916 famine was big business, as was indicated by the leading role taken by Meikle Brothers, the colony's premier private firm—pioneer settlers used to say that Southern Rhodesia contained 'nothing but Tom Meikle and white ants'.[21] The chief attraction for traders was the chance to buy cattle in return for grain, which deprived Africans of scarce cattle, depressed their price, failed to supply the poor, and encouraged traders to concentrate on relatively wealthy areas like Gutu and Gwanda rather than impoverished regions like Ndanga and the northern borderlands where famine was most acute. Nevertheless, private enterprise supplied large quantities of grain, far exceeding those made available in any previous famine. In Gutu District, for example, 13 000-14 000 bags were supplied during 1916, chiefly by private enterprise. In Buhera sub-district traders supplied 5 000-6 000 bags of grain and took away 2 480 cattle. In Insiza, where cattle prices were higher, 5 000 bags were supplied and 1 300 cattle sold. Africans in Bulalima-Mangwe sold some 4 000 of their 32 000 cattle, receiving over 6 000 bags of grain. In Gwanda the traders bought over 2 500 cattle with grain imported from the Transvaal.[22] No government relief was needed in Gwanda, and that was the general pattern in Matabeleland and the core areas of Mashonaland. In Chilimanzi District, for example, the government sold only 220 bags during the year — compared with some 3 000 supplied by traders — and had difficulty in disposing of its stocks.[23] Even in peripheral areas like Wankie and Chibi private enterprise generally supplied twice as much grain as the government. The chief exception, as always, was Ndanga.

Grain prices were lower and more stable in 1916 than in 1912, implying more efficient markets. Minimum wholesale white maize prices in Salisbury were approximately 15s. a bag at the beginning of 1916, fell to 12s. in May and rose again to 15s. in December, compared with 20s., 15s., and 24s., at equivalent months in 1912.[24] The fluctuation was little over 10 per cent on either side of the mean, compared with 25 per cent in 1912. In the countryside, traders bought African maize in the distant Mrewa District in May 1916 at up to 6s. a bag and paid roughly twice as much in Selukwe District in August.[25] Between May and August selling prices ranged between 17s. 6d. and 22s. 6d. in Belingwe and Gutu Districts, reaching 26s. in Melsetter District in September.[26] That was the highest cash price recorded anywhere during 1916 and was only half the peak price of 1912.

Cash prices, however, were often less significant than the relative price of grain as against cattle. Although the colony now had many more cattle than in 1912, stock prices were partly kept up by exports, which began in 1916 in response to a large and undiscriminating wartime demand.[27] The price of slaughter cattle in the Salisbury market during 1916 ranged between 30s. and 37s. 6d. per 100 lb. as against 37s. 6d. and 50s. during

1912,[28] which meant that cattle prices had fallen slightly less than grain prices, while showing a similar tendency to stabilize. Both trends were somewhat to the advantage of Africans seeking grain, but cattle prices in the countryside varied so enormously in terms of grain that generalization is barely possible. The most common price during 1916 was two or three bags of grain per beast. The quantities bartered in each district suggest that. The Native Commissioner in Hartley wrote that 3-5 bags per beast was normal but that stock prices had dropped by up to half during the year. In Charter the average price for a cow was £3, or about three or four bags of grain. In Gwanda a beast fetched between one and four bags, depending on its size.[29] The exchange of one beast for one bag of grain was often taken as the benchmark of extortionate famine prices, but was reported in 1916 only in southern Mashonaland, where disease restricted the movement of cattle and deterred traders from accepting them, thus making the famine especially serious. Between May and December 1916 traders acquired some 32 000 of the 446 060 cattle which Africans had owned in 1915.[30]

Famine was a means by which Europeans accumulated capital from Africans, but, conversely, their ability to do so resulted from the economic power they had already accumulated. One indication of this was their role in the production of maize, which occupied 86 per cent of their cultivated land. In 1915 Europeans had produced 914 926 bags of maize and exported 346 855 bags at prices as low as 7s. a bag, owing to heavy transport costs and competition in world markets.[31] It was not surprising, therefore, that when African crops failed in 1916 traders were so quick to transfer the European surplus to the African market. Southern Rhodesia exported only 51 259 bags of European-grown maize in 1916.[32] Famine was indeed good business.

It is less clear how far the famine itself was due to the European presence. Earlier famines showed little evidence that the effects of land alienation had so impoverished Africans as to make them more susceptible to famine than before. Rather, the famines of 1903 and 1912 resembled those of the nineteenth century. So did that of 1916: it was a famine of the peripheries where European impact was least. Estimates of African grain production per capita do not show a declining trend at this time.[33] Yet there were indications that the burden of White settlement was increasing. African land pressure was greatest in Matabeleland, where in 1915 only 36 per cent of Africans lived in the Reserves, as against 65 per cent in Mashonaland.[34] Because the status of individual areas changed frequently, comparable statistics are scarce, but since 1912 there had been a gradual and widespread, although not universal, movement of Africans from alienated land to Reserves, normally driven by refusal to accept the tenancy terms demanded by landowners, compounded by growing human and animal populations. This movement did not occur in the peripheral areas of Mashonaland, where there was little settlement, but it was evident in more central districts such as Makoni, where between 1911 and 1916 the number of Africans living on alienated land declined from 4 503 to 4 020 while the number inhabiting Reserves increased from 16 201 to 18 924.[35] In Matabeleland the process was marked and universal. In Matopo District, for example, the number of Africans living on alienated land fell between 1912 and 1916 from 9 954 to 7 700 while the Reserve population rose from 6 650 to 7 600; the balance mainly occupied land earmarked for Europeans, whose residents increased from 843 to 1 700.[36] Similar statistics could be quoted for Nyamandhlovu, Bubi, and Bulalima-Mangwe, while almost all rural Africans in Bulawayo and Mzingwane districts were already tenants on European estates.[37]

This process had two possible connections with famine. First, the gradual movement of Africans to the more arid areas and poorer soils exposed them to greater risk of crop failure. This was evident in Charter District, where Africans were gradually pressed towards the lower eastern section of Buhera, whose administrator reported in 1918 that 'I have never yet seen a normal crop in the Reserve and although acreage cultivated increases there has never been sufficient food produced to carry the population from season to season for the past three years'.[38] Second, some Africans who remained on alienated land could no longer meet their food needs. 'No grain is bought in this District from natives', the Native Commissioner in Matopo reported in 1916 when describing the famine there, 'and even in good seasons natives do not always grow sufficient for their own requirements but rely on being able to purchase grain fairly cheaply from traders'.[39] Although at an early stage, the loss of subsistence autonomy even in normal seasons threatened sections of the African people.

If the famine of 1916 revealed subtle shifts in Southern Rhodesia's economy, it also provoked subtle changes in official famine policy. In 1912 the authorities had held in theory, if not always in practice, to rigorous principles of political economy. Only the incapacitated might receive free grain; others must pay for it with cash, stock, or migrant labour, lest they be pauperized. Supply must be left to private traders with a minimum of state interference and expenditure. The policy met both the interests of settlers and the administrative preferences of Sir William Milton. In 1914, however, Milton was succeeded as Administrato by F.P.D. (later Sir Drummond) Chaplin, an aristocratic conservative in a more paternalistic mould. 'In 1916', a settler politician later recalled,

....when the Government considered the matter of relief, letters came pouring in to the effect that no relief should be given, but rather that the native should turn out to work, and that relief should only be given in wages as a return for work. The Administrator had taken up the attitude that no Government could refuse relief when relief was necessary.[40]

Moreover, with the police committed to the war effort, control of famine relief lay with the Chief Native Commissioner, H.J. Taylor, whose buccaneering youth had been sobered by personal experience of famine relief in 1896, an experience which softened many hard men.[41] In 1912 Taylor had striven to moderate the rigours of Milton's policy. Now he had the chance to implement his own.

The most striking difference between the famine policy of 1916 and that of 1912 was that additional experience enabled officials to foresee the crisis and provide against it. In this respect the adminstration was well ahead of its counterparts elsewhere in British Africa at this time.[42] By March 1916 many Native Commissioners were examining growing crops, laying in stocks of grain, and instructing Chiefs to give advance warning of possible shortage.[43] The first instructions issued to officials at this time resembled those of 1912: food might be issued free only to the incapacitated; all others must pay on receipt or later; issues should be made close to a railway; the people should fetch the food from there.[44] In April, however, Taylor added further directions which shifted the emphasis in two ways.[45] First, Native Commissioners were instructed not to interfere where Africans could be supplied by private enterprise without being imposed upon, a directive which placed on officials a duty to ensure fair trading within their districts. A week earlier Taylor had visited Belingwe, learned that traders were overcharging, and ordered 200 bags of grain 'to supply immediate wants and fix a basis for traders prices'.[46] Whether the government should hold grain stocks to stabilize the market had long been disputed in India.[47] Taylor's directive settled the matter for Southern Rhodesia. The policy was pursued throughout the colony during 1916 and probably helped to reduce price fluctuations. 'As one of the principal store keepers had, without, in my opinion, adequate reasons, raised his price', the Native Commissioner in Belingwe reported in October, 'I obtained authority to purchase two loads of grain which has had the desired effect of keeping other store keepers within a reasonable margin of profit'.[48] Taylor's second innovation in April 1916 was to order that, although all grain was to be issued either against payment or on credit, nevertheless if repayment could not be made within a reasonable time, Native Commissioners should seek permission to write off the debt. This was the basis for what became in effect massive free issues of grain in Ndanga. Elsewhere the concession was applied cautiously, pressure for repayment remained intense, and Africans often refused grain offered on credit because of the expected burden of repayment. But the approach had subtly changed:

> The sale of grain to Natives in the Bulawayo District has been left almost entirely to private enterprise. The prices charged are reasonable and I have seen no reason to intervene with Government grain. There are however a certain number of cases where Natives are unable through poverty to purchase, and to whom I find it necessary to advance grain in the hope of repayment.[49]

On the other hand one innovation was *not* made in 1916. The chief difference between famine policy in Southern Rhodesia and in India was that Southern Rhodesia expected hungry men to leave home and work for private employers, whereas Indian famine policy centred on opening public works within famine-stricken regions. The Indian policy ensured that cash and labour remained within the famine area.[50] Such a scheme was proposed to Chaplin in March 1916 by the Rhodesia Agricultural Union, which suggested that famine labour be used to build roads. The idea, however, was that this should replace sales of grain, and the Administrator brushed it aside.[51] Conditions in Southern Rhodesia at this time differed from India's, for workers rather than jobs were scarce in Southern Rhodesia, whereas lack of employment was the core of India's famine problem. Moreover, Southern Rhodesia's administration was probably not yet capable of organizing extensive relief works, especially in wartime. Yet the policy of draining labour from famine areas was almost certainly pernicious.

Taylor later estimated that during the famine of 1916 not less than 130 000 Africans had received food relief from the 44 000 bags which the government supplied to needy districts, 30 479 of them going to Ndanga and Bikita and another 10 078 to other parts of southern and southeastern Mashonaland.[52] The operation was far larger than in previous famines, more fully accepted as a normal administrative function, and more effective. It was little affected by the war, except perhaps through a shortage of railway rolling-stock. Animal-drawn transport, on the other hand, remained a serious weakness, especially on the northern peripheries and in southern Mashonaland at the height of the dry season. Yet the only deaths probably caused directly by famine were those in Ndanga and the migrant labourers from Mount Darwin who died at Shamva. Smallpox was virtually absent, perhaps owing to a mass vaccination campaign in 1914, and only scurvy is known to have caused increased mortality.[53] Taylor claimed that the famine had been the worst since the British occupation and that only government action had prevented thousands of deaths from starvation.[54] From what we have seen, that seems exaggerated. But Taylor was thinking of Ndanga.

The famine in Ndanga District and its Bikita sub-district in 1916 was the worst since 1896 and has had no subsequent parallel. Although the most populous District in the colony, Ndanga had never recovered from the famine of 1912. 'All the cattle were sold or killed', Native Commissioner Bazeley wrote of the south-western area in 1915. '....The older men are paupers, while the younger men are away at work, mostly in the Transvaal ... the greater part of them still owe for grain which was issued to them then.'[55] Added to this, every single season between 1912 and 1918 was abnormal. Early in 1915 unsatisfactory rains were compounded by locusts which ate the staple finger millet, making 1915 a famine year when government relief was necessary. This relief was ended in January 1916 in the hope that the rains would make wild produce available. Instead they failed completely and Bazeley predicted 'the worst famine known since the Occupation. Even now they are mainly subsisting on wild fruits and vegetables.'[56] When grain arrived in April for distribution to the south of the District, the people were already too weak to fetch it from Ndanga. Touring the Bikita sub-district at that time, Bazeley's assistant, H.N. Watters, found that only the higher areas had any crops; in the lowveld well over 10 000 people would need relief food within a month. He asked for 900 bags of grain immediately.[57] The government would have to supply it, for the District was too poor to attract traders. 'Their cattle had been seriously reduced in number and there was very little demand for them', Bazeley later explained, 'so that there was no assistance to be expected from private individuals'.[58]

The main relief operation began in May, when Bazeley estimated 'that nine tenths of the natives in the district have no food and will have to depend on the Government to save their lives'.[59] The officials found that feeding depots at Ndanga and Bikita were as much as they could handle. Most information is available for Bikita. It was a mud-brick-and-thatch station, high up on a spur of Hanyanga Mountain, where Watters, his family, a clerk, and two policemen lived in lonely authority, Watters being greeted with clapped hands whenever he emerged from his office.[60] Several times a week, especially when food convoys arrived from distant Fort Victoria, he rode down the mountain for an hour to the feeding depot, which was run by two African messengers, both heirs to local chieftainships. In principle they sold grain at 24s. a bag to cover cost, transport, and handling charges. In practice applicants had no cash and Watters refused cattle because of the difficulty of looking after them. Instead he issued grain on credit, listing the cattle owned by recipients or extracting promises to undertake migrant labour once the famine ended. 'I have no fear that the loans.... will be repaid at the earliest opportunity', he assured Bazeley.[61] Applicants with nothing to offer in return were given a double handful of maize. Watters issued 388 bags of grain during May, far less than was needed. In June he distributed 1 266 bags, in July 2 225, in August 2 465, in September 2 378, in October 2 004, and in November 4 138 — a total of 14 864 bags. In the same period Ndanga issued 14 869 bags, plus another 1 087 in December.[62] At Bikita almost every bag was distributed as soon as it arrived, for the depot attracted both a permanent population and thousands of people who came, often 'in a fainting condition due to hunger', to await the arrival of grain.[63] In August, when transport broke down and no grain arrived for a fortnight, some 5 000 people camped there. 'No one who has not actually been here can understand all that this means', Watters wrote later. 'Many times the natives have rushed me to get possession of grain, and this to the number of 4,000 or more at a time.'[64] In October, however, good early rains fell, so that Watters could skilfully bring the relief operation to an end during November by issuing an especially large quantity and then abruptly closing the depot, making it both necessary and possible for recipients to return home and sow crops for the new season.

In financial terms, the cost was heavy. On 16 November Africans in Bikita owed £16 980 for grain received on credit. In Ndanga the sum at the end of 1916 was £17 491.[65] Six years later a total of £7 879 was still unpaid in Ndanga and Bazeley's successor asked for it to be written off. He denounced 'the weak and extravagant policy' followed in 1916, 'when supplies of grain on credit, were literally thrown at any native who applied for it'. Some, he claimed, had paid their taxes by selling grain received on credit.[66] Chief Native Commissioner Taylor denied it. 'When thousands of natives asking for relief are dealt with by small staffs', he wrote, 'it is unavoidable that mistakes may occur: but I am not prepared to admit that any large number of natives obtained grain improperly'.[67] The surprising point, perhaps, was that so much of the debt was repaid.

Both Watters and Bazeley claimed that not a single African died from hunger, but Bazeley also wrote that 'The stamina of the natives was undoubtedly affected by the famine but comparatively few deaths at the kraals were reported', so that complete certainty on the point is impossible.[68] In either case, the prevention of mass starvation by the supply of roughly 2 500 tons of grain was a remarkable administrative achievement, for on this occasion other survival mechanisms could scarcely have prevented many hundreds or thousands of deaths. As Watters wrote, 'This has undoubtedly been the worst famine in the memory of the oldest natives of this district'.[69] He remained at Bikita for many years, took a special interest in medical work, and is said to have been known by Africans as Maponese, 'Saviour'.[70] In July 1916, at the height of the famine, he had asked to be released to join the forces.[71]

# CHAPTER 7

## Transitional Famine, 1922

Whereas the famines of 1903, 1912 and 1916 had been largely of the pre-colonial type, that of 1922 showed clear signs of transition to a new pattern.[1] No single district suffered so severely as Ndanga had suffered in 1916, but scarcity, famine relief, and a scattering of deaths took place in almost every region, and they occurred at a time when the colony possessed enough grain to feed all its inhabitants and to export a little. That people starved when food existed was partly because they had been impoverished by the operation of the commercial economy, especially the collapse of cattle prices. In that sense, the famine of 1922 was a step towards the capitalist famines of the later colonial period, as also in the sense that the official relief effort in 1922 was the largest the authorities ever mounted. That some scores of people nevertheless died was largely because reliance on animal transport made the new techniques of famine control imperfect at a time of transition when indigenous techniques were weakening.

One symptom of the change was that the famine of 1922 was the first of the colonial period that was not the climax of several bad years but followed a series of good seasons and a single bad one. Both Salisbury and Bulawayo had enjoyed average or above-average rainfall in every summer between 1917/18 and 1920/1, while estimated African grain production per head in the early 1920s was at its highest point of the twentieth century.[2] In 1921/2, however, total rainfall was disastrous. Salisbury received only 58 per cent of its average and Fort Victoria 57 per cent — in both cases the lowest figures since records began — while Bulawayo enjoyed 65 per cent and Hope Fountain, slightly to the south, only 41 per cent. Even well-watered Umtali in the eastern highlands had by 11 April 1922 received less than 250 mm of rain during the entire season. Such widespread failure was unprecedented. It came, moreover, in an especially cruel manner, for the rainfall in November and December 1921 was generally good and the crops looked promising, but the rain ceased late in December and the growing crops shrivelled in the fields. The result was that estimated African grain production per head fell to 1,50 bags, as against 4,30 bags in 1920, 4,22 in 1921, and 4,32 in 1923.[3] When senior officials discussed the situation on 10 April, relief operations were already in progress in Gwanda. They were needed immediately to the south and south-east of Bulawayo, where crops had failed and cattle were unsaleable; in the 'famine belt', as it was becoming known, of southern Mashonaland and the Sabi valley; and in the north of Inyanga District, where some 7 000 people administered by the luckless Bazeley had suffered complete harvest failure.[4] The officials expected that operations in Matabeleland would have to be extended later to Bulawayo, Bubi, and Belingwe Districts; that Umtali (with only a 25 per cent harvest) would need aid; and — perhaps most significantly — that relief would be necessary in the south of Gutu District in south-central Mashonaland, an area prosperous in the late nineteenth century but now increasingly famine-prone, especially in its lower southern section.[5] Gutu was already the centre of a modest smallpox epidemic, with 122 cases and 2 deaths during March. Two months later the disease killed 21 people in the Wedza Reserve of Marandellas District, but as 1922 continued and the famine worsened, so vaccination and isolation brought this epidemic to an end. It was the only epidemic experienced during 1922, although there was also the usual increase in cases of scurvy.[6]

During March crop failure became likely throughout Central Africa. In parts of southern Mozambique, for example, the famine of 1922 is said to have killed up to one-third of the population.[7] Anticipations of crisis raised the price of grain. Hitherto it had been very low, owing to post-war depression and the difficulty of selling the record crop of 1921 on the world market. Late in 1921 some Africans in Matabeleland were unable to sell surplus grain at any price.[8] In February 1922 the wholesale price of white maize in Salisbury was 8s. 6d. a bag, compared to 15s. at the beginning of 1916. By late March 1922, however, the price had soared to 14s. It remained at that level throughout the winter and then rose to 20s. during October and November, when the famine was most acute, before levelling out at 18s. in December. These fluctuations — a 40 per cent variation on either side of the mean, compared with 25 per cent in 1912 and 10 per cent in 1916 — indicated both the severity of the shortage and its sudden occurrence amid otherwise favourable years.[9] This was also apparent in Southern Rhodesia's exports of European-grown maize, which reached 488 665 bags in 1919/20 and 346 556 in 1920/1 before falling to 32 556 in 1921/2 and then rising again to 789 411 in 1922/3.[10] Clearly the smaller grain crop produced by European farmers in 1922 was redirected from the export market to the more profitable African domestic market. As in 1916, famine was good business, especially for those who held their crops until the end of the year, when maize was selling in Gwelo for up to 30s. a bag.[11]

For Africans, however, the true severity of the famine lay not in high grain prices but in low cattle prices. Stock prices had fallen in earlier famines, but they had been supported by European attempts to build up herds, African desires to recover from rinderpest, and the temporary

69

demands of the First World War. By the early 1920s, however, the colony was largely restocked, while the world meat market collapsed in the depression of 1921-2. During 1922 slaughter cattle sold in the Salisbury market for between 20s. and 27s. 6d. per 100 lb., as against 30s. and 37s. 6d. in 1916 and 37s. 6d. and 50s. in 1912.[12] 'The price of beef is fast approaching the vanishing point', a newspaper complained in July.[13] In Gwanda District, where Ndebele kings had pastured their herds, cattle sold in January 1922 at the traditional famine price of one beast for a bag of grain. This price recurred frequently during the year,[14] together with cash values of between £1 and £3 per head. 'A beast could not always be sold for as much as its hide would have realised three years ago', the Native Commissioner in Belingwe commented.[15] In many areas cattle were simply unsaleable, either because traders could find no market for them or because East Coast Fever prevented them being moved.

The famine of 1922 was transitional not only because it was partly due to market fluctuations but because traditional famine-prevention techniques were less effective than before. That a single harvest failure should have caused serious and widespread shortage, often in the earliest months of the year, implied that indigenous storage systems no longer functioned successfully. Probably they had never been fully effective, and Native Commissioners disagreed as to whether storage had become neglected, but some thought it a logical consequence of commercialization. In Mrewa, for example, the knowledgeable 'Wiri' Edwards wrote in 1920, 'Nowadays the natives do not carry large reserves of food, all surplus over and above their own requirements being sold to traders'. His colleague in Mazoe agreed: 'Natives do not now keep much more than is required for the year'.[16] The experienced Superintendent of Natives in Bulawayo, H.M.G. Jackson, attributed the scarcity of 1922 to the very prosperity of recent years. 'Their grain pits and corn bins had been allowed to become unduly depleted', he explained. '....They were misled by a succession of good harvests, by a season which had opened with exceptional promise and by the inflated value of their cattle. These last became almost unsaleable.'[17] His equally experienced namesake in Gwelo, S.N.G. Jackson, pointed to insecurity of tenure, which 'has to a great extent caused the Matabele to discontinue the use of pits'.[18] The Native Commissioner in Gutu blamed the famine relief issued in the past. 'It was reported to me a few days ago that a native had sold a bag of rapoko to a farmer for £1', he complained. 'On being asked by the farmer why he was selling grain when the crops were bad, (he) replied "It is quite allright, the Government will let us have grain when we are short."'[19] This was probably not a common attitude, but a generation of grain sales to European traders may have made many Africans dependent on this source of cash and encouraged them to balance well-stocked bins against immediate profits. The only District with ample reserves from 1921, Bulalima-Mangwe, was said to have them for lack of buyers.[20] Native Commissioners had complained for several years that Africans sold grain at low prices immediately after harvest and had to buy it back later at famine rates. These complaints were especially common during 1922. 'In Bepura's Area where the natives parted with hundreds of bags to traders at 6/- a bag, they are now re-purchasing grain at 25/-', it was reported from Lomagundi in November.[21] Many officials blamed improvidence. Some banned traders from Native Reserves when harvests failed. A few realized the urgent need for cash which probably lay behind early sales. 'To sit with the tax pound in the purse and face a famine requires the mental discipline of a fanatic', an official wrote,[22] but perhaps all it really required was the existing penalties for not paying tax. S.N.G. Jackson's account was balanced. 'During the past 2 years', he wrote early in 1923, 'the restriction of markets for cattle and labour have caused the natives to dispose of more grain than they should, in order to meet their financial obligations to the Government and to their landlords, and also to secure clothing, blankets, salt, etc.'[23]

Other indigenous defences against famine may also have been weakening. Forest produce, for example, remained an important resource in lowveld areas like south-eastern Mtoko District and the Sabi and Lundi valleys, but it was seldom mentioned on the Mashonaland highveld, had always been less important in Matabeleland, and was less central than usual even in the Zambezi valley, where the drought was so bad that some wild species bore no fruit.[24] In contrast with earlier years, 'The able bodied among the community scattered, after the reaping of such crops as were reapable, to seek work and barter fowls and tobacco & c for grain', as an official in the valley reported, 'while the old and infirm were left to search the veldt for what nourishment the wilderness would yield in the way of edible fruits and herbs'.[25]

As survival techniques, foraging and migrant labour were incompatible. That labour generally took precedence in 1922 was another indication of transition in famine strategies. On this occasion famine undoubtedly increased the supply of labour throughout the territory. There were still peripheral areas like the Sabi valley where men insisted on remaining with their families during famine. A few prosperous peasant areas such as Makoni may have been able to avoid migration. Generally, however, seeking work was a more widespread response to famine than ever before. 'Numbers of youths and small boys, who would not ordinarily come into the labour market for some years, offered their services to earn money for their families owing to the straightened

71

circumstances they found themselves in from the effect of the drought and the continued slump in the price of cattle', the Native Commissioner in Bulalima-Mangwe reported.[26] For the first time, young men in Urungwe were observed to take their wives with them to workplaces. For the first time, too, there was an over-supply of labour during the drought of 1922. 'The dry season has hit the (European) farmers', a missionary reported from Marandellas, 'and they have dismissed their natives by scores and in one case, near here, by hundreds.'[27] Real wages in agriculture and mining averaged only half their value of 1914.[28] In Inyanga District, where Europeans had been especially greedy for land, Africans worked for White farmers in return for food only. In Chiweshe Reserve, north of Salisbury, they did the same for African farmers lucky with the rains.[29]

Exchange remained a major survival technique. As soon as harvest failure appeared likely, people from Empandeni in the south-west 'made long journeys to buy what they can elsewhere of last year's crop'.[30] In more fortunate areas a lively trade took place among Africans after harvest, even where Europeans could find little grain to buy. People from habitual deficit areas like the lowveld of Bikita drove stock into the highlands to exchange for grain. The trade in salt from the Sabi valley flourished. New forms of exchange appeared. During the famine of 1912 Christians near the Mutambara Mission in Melsetter District had copied the irrigation practices of their Afrikaner neighbours. Ten years later their crops were an important famine resource and the Native Commissioner dreamed of the Sabi becoming 'a second Nile Valley'.[31] Parts of the newly-settled Gwaai Reserve in Matabeleland acted as a local granary. Yet it was clear early in the year that many Africans would depend on European traders. 'Numbers of farmers, traders and others are importing stocks of grain and depositing them in various parts of the district for sale to natives', the Native Commissioner reported from Ndanga at the end of April.[32] Next month he added that the prices asked were exorbitant. The official in Mzingwane had already reported one case of profiteering during March and feared that it might become common. Many of his colleagues agreed, especially in view of low cattle prices.

In the event, only four of the colony's thirty-six Districts — Mrewa, Mazoe, Salisbury, and Bulalima-Mangwe — survived the year without relief.[33] That scarcity occurred in areas with little land alienation as well as those with many settlers suggested that White settlement was still only a subsidiary cause of famine. Since 1912 the population of Native Reserves had grown by about 100 000, while the number of Africans living on European property had remained roughly stable.[34] Yet these figures concealed many local evictions, especially in eastern and central Mashonaland and central Matabeleland. In Inyanga District, for example, the number of Africans on European land decreased between 1916 and 1922 from 12 329 to 10 793. In Umtali the equivalent figures were 11 874 and 9 627. In Charter they were 9 645 and 5 265.[35] In these cases, movement to lower, more arid, and already overcrowded land probably worsened the famine of 1922, but it is unlikely to have compared, as a cause, with Umtali's rainfall of less than 250 mm. In Matabeleland, similarly, the number of Africans on alienated land in famine-stricken Matopo District declined between 1916 and 1922 from 7 700 to 5 800, while those in the Reserves increased from 7 600 to 10 290,[36] but an even greater movement occurred in Bulalima-Mangwe, where there was no famine in 1922.[37] Native Commissioners at this time saw a land problem as just beginning and expected it to take the form of overstocking in the Reserves. Africans had more urgent fears, especially in Manicaland and in Matabeleland, where political leaders regularly demanded more land.[38] Yet the fact that estimated African grain production per head peaked in the early 1920s suggests that European settlement had as yet done little damage to African agriculture.

As the likelihood of near-universal famine became clear during April, the Native Department prepared a relief programme, drawing on its now considerable experience. As before, policy was to rely wherever possible on private enterprise. 'Supplies of grain', Chief Native Commissioner Taylor was told, 'should not be made in localities where the local traders are selling grain to natives at reasonable prices as it is desired not to interfere with bona-fide and legitimate trading and it is very desirable that Government relief should be restricted to the smallest possible amount compatible with the welfare of the native.'[39] Yet Taylor estimated that private traders would supply only 22 000 of the 80 000 bags needed. The government would have to provide the rest. In May it earmarked £35 000 for famine relief, ordered the first 10 000 bags from the (European) Farmers' Cooperative in Salisbury, and began to stockpile grain in vulnerable areas:

> Depots have been made in the Sabi Valley and it is hoped by the end of June that there will be up to 500 bags of Government grain in the district. Information from all sources has been sought. Missionaries, farmers and others have been asked to supply this and are agreed that no real shortage will arise until about August or September: but it will be seen nothing is being left to chance that the natives will go short or that they may be unduly exploited by sellers, as the 500 bags mentioned above will prevent this.[40]

Following the precedents of 1916, government grain supplies had two functions: to stabilize prices and prevent exploitation, and to supply extreme need where private enterprise failed. Although Taylor denied that food had been distributed recklessly in 1916 and insisted that 'elimination of the undeserving should be gradual rather than that any risk should be run of really impoverished natives dying of starvation',[41] nevertheless the fact that £7 879 was still owed for grain issued in 1916 let him to warn the authorities in southern Mashonaland that stricter controls were essential. 'One general principle is applicable certainly', he wrote, 'i.e. to avoid the accumulation of large debts'.[42] 'An effort was made to run the relief measures on strictly business lines', the Superintendent of Natives in Fort Victoria later reported, 'the underlying principle being to issue grain in comparatively small quantities to relieve the immediate necessities of families.'[43] Ndanga's debt for issues made in 1922 was £3 784.[44]

The chief innovation in famine policy in 1922 was the organization of public works on the Indian model, an innovation necessary in 1922 because, for the first time, private employers could not provide work for all those seeking it. Public works meant building roads, partly the main road from Salisbury to Bulawayo but mainly dirt roads in the Reserves for the motor cars increasingly owned by officials and settlers. Those employed were paid in food. There was resistance to the programme in prosperous Makoni District, but motor roads were built to almost every part of Bikita District and similar reports were made elsewhere. The programme cost the government £3 250.[45]

These measures were prepared in April and May and were gradually implemented more widely as winter deepened and reports of scarcity multiplied. In June the chief need was in Matabeleland, Manicaland and southern Mashonaland. In July the first reports arrived of deaths from starvation in the Zambezi valley.[46] Relief issues in Charter and Gutu Districts of west-central Mashonaland began in August and Taylor made an urgent visit to Mount Darwin, where the Native Commissioner had reported acute scarcity in the Dande. Issues began there and in Wankie during September, when the Native Commissioner in Chilimanzi also reported that 'practically all natives are in a state of semi-starvation' and began to arrange food distribution.[47] In October, as the European population voted for Southern Rhodesia's internal self-government, the demand for relief among hungry Africans grew almost everywhere, while the price of grain began its rapid increase. October, however, also saw exceptionally early and heavy rains throughout the colony. Wild foods appeared. The Native Commissioner in Belingwe began to close his feeding depots. In November the rain faltered and the demand grew further. 'As soon as a wagon load of grain arrives it is disposed of', an official wrote from Sipolilo in the extreme north. '....Food, more food, and still more food is the cry.' A month later he reported eleven deaths from starvation,[48] but the general situation was increasingly patchy, with relief needed for the first time in Wedza but an end predicted within a fortnight in Bikita. So acute was the crisis in the Dande during January 1923 that Chief Chizwiti burned to death a man supposedly responsible for holding up the rains by defiling the 'wife' of the rain-spirit Karuva.[49] By then, however, the general demand for food was falling off quickly, an excellent harvest seemed assured, and relief operations ceased almost everywhere. The last government grain was issued in Sipolilo in March 1923.

The relief operation was the largest yet mounted. By 31 March 1923 the government had supplied 67 931 bags of grain, compared with 44 000 in 1916.[50] This was no 'token effort', as has been alleged of official relief in Northern Nigeria, but nor was it necessarily a sign that the people were being pauperized.[51] It was more an indication that the government was becoming more efficient, that its relief system was slowly replacing earlier methods of famine control, and that European traders were less effective on this occasion because they were less eager to acquire cattle. They were still the most important external suppliers of grain in Matabeleland and central Mashonaland during 1922, but they were less active in the peripheries and complaints of overcharging were more common. Consequently, in contrast to 1916, when two-thirds of official relief went to Ndanga District, government supplies in 1922 were more evenly spread among 32 Districts, the largest recipients (to 31 December 1922) being Ndanga (5 360 bags), Melsetter (5 222), and Belingwe (5 020). The total cost of the operation to 31 March 1923 was £72 302. Of this, £23 289 had already been recovered in cash and £13 766 in cattle. Africans owed another £39 260 for grain on credit. Taylor calculated that if all was repaid, the government would make a profit of £5 310 on the operation.[52] How much was repaid is unclear, but Inyanga District still had £338 outstanding at the end of 1928.[53] European settlers and their newspapers, which were not quick to praise the Native Department, were nevertheless impressed by its efficiency during 1922. 'The Native Department has done wonders with the famine relief', a correspondent wrote from Melsetter; 'I don't think there have been many, if any, cases of death from starvation amongst the natives, which speaks volumes for the splendid organisation of the Department, especially when consideration is taken of the distance from the rail and the state of the roads the food had to be transported over.'[54]

Transport was especially difficult in Melsetter because, apart from the usual inadequacy of roads and of grazing for draught-animals during the winter, the distance from railhead was especially great there — 222 km to the furthest distribution point — and donkeys were used rather than oxen, for fear of disease. Transport also obstructed aid to the Zambezi valley:

> When consulted in August last (i.e. 1922), these people refused Government Famine Relief on account of the great distance (a journey of from four to five days through large tracts waterless in the winter season) that lies between this station and their country. There is no possibility of conveying grain to them on account of Tetse fly, and the steep and rugged nature of the Escarpment.[55]

Early in 1923 a consignment of grain was delayed for a month in this area by the flooded Mkwadzi river. There was also difficulty in supplying remote parts of the southern lowveld, but not on the scale of earlier famines. This region was one of many opened to motor transport at this time, but although motor cars enabled officials to visit threatened areas speedily, there is no indication that relief grain was transported by motor vehicles in 1922. The age of the lorry — a vital weapon against famine — had not yet come.

To demonstrate that a baby or an elderly person dying during a famine has died as a result of that famine is extremely difficult. For this reason, Taylor refused to admit that anyone had died as a result of famine during 1922,[56] but the evidence in his subordinates' reports was against him. It suggested, rather, a few score deaths in a very clear pattern. Whereas scarcity was widespread, deaths were confined to peripheral areas and especially weak and vulnerable groups. Of some 47 deaths attributed by Native Commissioners to famine, the largest number, 17, took place in Buhera sub-district, whose lowveld sloped down to the river Sabi.[57] Slightly fewer occurred in the section of the Zambezi valley administered from Sipolilo, where the official described the victims as those too old or young to fetch grain.[58] Another seven elderly people died in that part of the valley governed from Urungwe.[59] All the remaining deaths were in peripheral districts. The elderly suffered especially. In Ndanga, for example, 'Many of the older natives coming to the office for grain, arrive in an emaciated and exhausted state, and meal has to be supplied to them to enable them to recover otherwise the mealies issued to them are liable to be ravenously devoured with fatal results.'[60] Even where there were no deaths, the weak suffered most, as at Empandeni:

> Some of the people, the children especially, are beginning to suffer from want, but the distress is not acute. Should it become so the Government will come to their relief. A good many natives have large herds of cattle, and as they can exchange these for grain, they are in no danger of feeling the pangs of hunger. But others are really poor, and it is they — and in particular their children — who are likely to suffer.[61]

Although government relief was the most efficient to date, it attracted more humanitarian criticism than before. This probably indicated that European expectations of the government were rising. Criticism focused on two points. In December 1922 the distinguished Methodist missionary, John White, complained from Marandellas District that 'The Government offers assistance on terms that do little for the most needy cases. Men that are too old to work on Government jobs, who have no money or cattle, should be assisted or some may actually die of starvation.'[62] Taylor replied with some justice that his organization did make special provision for the weak, but White, who thought the famine the worst he had seen during 28 years in Southern Rhodesia, launched a local relief operation, overspending, as his biographer put it, 'with a noble recklessness'.[63] An African recalled:

> Right through the whole of Rhodesia, people were dying. Many men ran to the Native Commissioner. Except in Marandellas District, there were not many who got their help from the Native Commissioner, because of this simple reason: People who first met him and asked for help were told to work on the roads first, which go through the Reserve.
> On that account many people left his help and went to Baba White for assistance....
> Women who had no husbands — he would give to them first. He did not wait for something from them, but gave them the mealie meal as a free gift. Even to those who were able to return him something, Baba White did not ask first how much money each man had got.[64]

'Though all promised to pay him back', another African remembered, 'when the time of plenty came, only a few refunded him for his outlay'.[65] This admiration of generosity rather than calculation in time of need sprang from the belief among Africans that their rulers had reciprocal obligations towards them. As a missionary pictured it, 'Must not they who exercise authority upon them justify their existence and their time-honoured title of benefactors of men?'[66] Officials would have called this pauperization. But similar thinking underlay the second line of criticism, which centred on *mucheneko,* the practice of issuing famine relief on credit to be repaid later. The problem was that the grain was charged at famine rates but repaid when prices had returned to normal levels. 'The natives have to pay 19/- a bag cash for the grain lent them 5/6 per bag more than Government paid for it. Grain is selling at 14/- a bag fast dropping in price', Archdeacon Upcher complained in April 1923.[67] Here too the government trusted in political economy.

Nevertheless, the authorities held their own autopsy on the crisis. In November 1922 Taylor asked his officials for suggestions to prevent recurrent famine. Three were advanced. One was that each District should build up a cash fund as an insurance against dearth,[68] but nothing came of this. A second was that every African family should be compelled to fill and seal a reserve grain bin to be opened only in famine years. Although many officials thought this impracticable, the Superintendent of Natives in Fort Victoria, C.L. Carbutt, issued such instructions to those under his authority.[69] More support greeted a third suggestion, that Africans should be required to grow drought-resistant crops, especially cassava, which was widely cultivated in neighbouring Mozambique but not in Southern Rhodesia. This now became official policy,[70] as in many other African colonies at this period. For the first time, the Southern Rhodesian authorities turned their minds from the relief of famine to its prevention.

# CHAPTER 8

## Depression and Scarcity, 1933

By the early 1930s the pattern of periodic food scarcity in Southern Rhodesia had changed decisively from that of the nineteenth century and the early colonial period.[1] The main change was that scarcity no longer caused identifiable deaths. Relatively brief periods of acute starvation gave way to rather longer periods of non-fatal scarcity. The location of scarcity also changed. Early colonial famines (apart from the special case of 1896) had concentrated either in the peripheries (1903, 1922) or in southern Mashonaland (1912, 1916). From the early 1930s, however, Matabeleland — so prosperous in the later nineteenth century — became the region of recurrent scarcity, chiefly because its resistance to drought had been weakened by massive alienation of land on the highveld and the gradual eviction of Africans to arid lowveld, whose effects began to be felt seriously at this time. Whereas early colonial famines centred where the European impact was least, later colonial scarcity concentrated where the European impact was greatest.

A third change probably accompanied these, but lack of evidence makes this little more than speculation. In the past, harvest failure was generally localized, for the transport of food from surplus to deficit areas was difficult. If an area was hungry, most people there were hungry; if its harvest was abundant, most rejoiced. The people of a locality fasted or feasted together. Once food could easily be transported from surplus to deficit areas, however, not only did starvation become less common, but so did surfeit. Famine and feast both gave way to a more even *geographical* distribution of food. *Socially,* however, distribution may have become less equal. Whereas both rich and poor had fasted and feasted, now food was regularly available to those who could afford it and regularly scarce for those who could not. As famine became less acute, malnutrition may have become more common. This is speculation because nutritional studies began exceptionally late in Southern Rhodesia, scarcely before the 1950s. The high levels of malnutrition then found may well have existed, unrecorded, at earlier periods. But logic suggests that the nutritional status of the poor may well have declined under colonial rule.

These changes did not result from changes in Southern Rhodesia's rainfall. The relatively arid period which had begun at the end of the nineteenth century and reached its lowest point before the First World War recorded a second trough in the late 1920s and early 1930s. Only thereafter did rainfall generally improve, although with dry spells in the late 1940s and late 1950s. Nor was the end of 'famine that killed' a result of improvements in African farming. Rather, it occurred at precisely the moment — in the late 1920s and early 1930s — when African agricultural production declined significantly. Although there has been much debate about this,[2] the attached Table shows that before 1930 annual African grain production consistently averaged over three bags per head, except during the acute drought before the First World War. After 1930, however, it fell permanently below that level. The change was not dramatic, but it was clear and consistent. The chief reasons for the decline were the limited land available to Africans and the increase of their population, an increase estimated — perhaps overestimated — at the very high level of 3,1 per cent a year during the 1930s, rising to a peak of 3,5 per cent a year in the early 1950s.[3] The most important point about the history of famine in twentieth-century Zimbabwe is not that it was largely controlled during the later colonial period, for it had largely been controlled before colonial rule. The important point was that rapid population growth was not allowed to make famine *more* common.

The ending of 'famine that killed' was not due to climatic change, African agriculture, or demography. It was due to the further development of the European-controlled commercial economy and its attendant administrative and transport systems. In effect, a capitalist system of famine control replaced the pre-capitalist system of the nineteenth century. The new system centred on European grain production, rail and

## Table
### ESTIMATED AFRICAN GRAIN PRODUCTION PER HEAD
(200 lb. bags, five-year annual averages)

| | |
|---|---|
| 1900-04 | 3,26 |
| 1909-13 | 3,11 |
| 1912-16 | 2,89 |
| 1914-18 | 3,01 |
| 1919-23 | 3,59 |
| 1924-28 | 3,32 |
| 1929-33 | 2,87 |
| 1934-38 | 2,68 |
| 1938-42 | 2,44 |
| 1943-47 | 2,69 |
| 1948-52 | 2,18 |
| 1953-57 | 2,96 |
| 1958-62 | 2,38 |

*Source:* P. Mosley, *The Settler Economies* (Cambridge, 1983), 72.

motor transport, a state-controlled marketing structure which also functioned as a system of famine relief, and the general growth and diversification of the economy which multiplied African opportunities for off-farm earnings. The cost of this system to Africans was their dependence on it. Instead of trusting to their grain bins, they had to rely on the Maize Control Board's silos.

These changes were not completed during the 1930s. The scarcity of 1933 — chosen as the worst of the decade, although not truly a famine year like those of the past — showed many similarities with pre-colonial and early colonial famines and contained many patterns of transition already observed in 1922. Yet the differences were more striking than the continuities. At root, capitalist scarcity replaced pre-capitalist famine in a pattern which has gradually happened throughout the world during the last four centuries.

* * * *

Two kinds of dearth dominated the decade after 1922. One was sporadic hunger in peripheral regions. In 1924 crops failed seriously in the Zambezi valley. Four years later they failed again there and in the lower parts of Mrewa, Mtoko, and Mount Darwin Districts, all of which needed government relief. The Zambezi valley suffered again during 1931, this time in common with the lowveld of southern Mashonaland. The other kind of scarcity was more ominous. Beginning late in 1925, the lower parts of Matabeleland entered a long drought which broadened in 1928 to cause harvest failure throughout the region.[4] Two relatively good years followed, but the rainfall declined again in 1930/1 to reach a new low point in the summer of 1932/3, when Bulawayo received 325 mm, only 54 per cent of its average and the lowest figure since the British occupation. Salisbury, by contrast, received 93 per cent of its average rainfall in 1932/3 and Fort Victoria 96 per cent. Locusts, which had returned sporadically during the 1920s, were very numerous during 1933, especially in Matabeleland, where a swarm fifty kilometres wide was reported from Nyamandhlovu during December.[5] They did surprisingly little damage, but conditions as a whole were bad enough to reduce estimated African grain production to 2,06 bags per head, compared with an average of 3,06 during the previous five years.[6] 'The year 1933', an African pastor in Matabeleland pronounced, 'was bad from its beginning to its end'.[7]

The badness was, however, localized. In central Mashonaland, for example, the Marandellas District blamed its poor crops on excessive rain. Generally the harvest in this region was not disastrous. European maize farmers in Mazoe District — the colony's leading maize producer — averaged 7,0 bags an acre, as against 7,6 for the 1930s as a whole.[8] By comparison, African growers in this district were said to average little over two bags an acre in 1933, although they still sold nearly 20 000 bags of grain to traders. Pressure on land in Mazoe was forcing a number of Africans to remove to less crowded peripheral areas like Mount Darwin. 'In many cases', the Native Commissioner reported, 'these were Natives who were dissatisfied with the terms under which they were living on alienated land or whose presence was no longer required by the land owner'.[9] In Lomagundi, similarly, the development of European tobacco farming obliged many Africans to leave ancestral land which they had hitherto continued to occupy despite formal alienation.[10] In Marandellas the Reserves were becoming seriously overcrowded, for their estimated population had increased since the famine of 1922 from 26 264 to 37 093.[11] After a generation of relative prosperity, land shortage was becoming a serious problem for some Shona.

Yet scarcity in Mashonaland in 1933 still concentrated chiefly in the vulnerable peripheries. In the east the worst-affected areas were Umtali, where 16 152 Africans were living on European property and the land problem was especially acute; the Chikwizo Reserve in the lowveld on the Portuguese border; around Mtoko, 'where lands are hopelessly worked out' and some government relief was necessary; and in the Dande, where locusts 'created havoc' and the people survived on famine foods.[12] Further south, Chief Chilimanzi had lost most of his highveld early in the century and the growing population in his Reserve — 12 703 in 1922, 18 036 in 1933 — made it a deficit area which needed 300 bags of government grain in 1933.[13] Chibi District had very poor crops but survived without government aid by means of good reserves, famine foods, and the sale of some 9 000 cattle.[14] The same was true in Ndanga and Bikita, where only the elderly and infirm needed famine relief — a remarkable improvement for the 'famine belt', due chiefly to the survival of grain stocks from the previous good season. The Sabi valley in Melsetter District, by contrast, had suffered several poor years, possessed no grain reserves, and experienced the most severe famine in the colony when drought and locusts destroyed the crops early in 1933. The valley-dwellers turned first to their neighbours in Portuguese territory, who were indebted to them for aid in 1922. Some worked there in return for food. Others took dried beef to trade, a new resource because cattle had not generally been kept in the valley before population growth had eradicated tsetse there. Another new resource was irrigated land, now amounting to over 160 ha. In October, however, government relief became necessary and Peter Nielsen, the enlightened Native Commissioner in Melsetter, faced the recurrent difficulty of transporting grain into the valley from the distant railhead at Umtali. By the end of the year he had supplied 400 bags to the Musikavanhu area where 'something like general and severe famine' reigned.[15]

It was assumed that there would be famine in the Sabi valley during any year of widespread drought. The same was true further north in the Zambezi valley, where crops were patchy and no government relief was needed but many people relied on wild produce. The scarcity in Matabeleland, by contrast, was ominous. Good rains early in the year virtually ceased on 25 January and within a month serious food shortage was anticipated. 'Crops are dying all round us', a missionary wrote from Hope Fountain on 3 March, 'and the veldt is as brown and dry as in the winter. Depression and gloom surround us on every side. Unemployment, both European and Native, is becoming an increasingly serious problem and with famine threatening us it seems that we have our share of trouble.'[16] Two deaths from marasmus and three from scurvy in Gwanda District were reported during March,[17] although they were not specifically attributed to drought. At this stage food reserves existed from 1932 and only Matopo, Belingwe, and Mtetengwe Districts expected to need relief later in the year. The risk seemed greatest in Matopo District, where the African population on alienated land had declined since 1922 from 5 800 to 3 150 while the numbers in Native Reserves had risen from 10 290 to 19 000.[18] Yet the first demands for relief came in August from Gwelo District, whose sparse reserves had been overstocked even in 1922. Gwelo suffered severe food shortage during 1933, many surviving for the last two or three months of the year on wild produce and locusts, while the government supplied grain on credit to the incapacitated. In October the Native Commissioner in Matopo 'met hundreds of natives ... clamouring for famine relief'. He referred them to private traders, who sold a thousand bags of grain to the needy. Some 15 per cent of Matopo's cattle died of poverty during the year,[19] a pattern which was common in Matabeleland in this and later droughts and was perhaps the clearest evidence of pressure on land. In Bulawayo District, where only 260 Africans could find space in the Reserves, every farm which granted grazing rights to African tenants was overstocked and between one-quarter and one-fifth of the cattle died.[20] Bulawayo needed small quantities of famine relief during November, as did Mzingwane District where there was no substantial Native Reserve at all. By then rain was falling everywhere in Matabeleland, breaking three years of drought, although for the present 'many natives are feeling the pinch of shortage of food and grain for planting purposes is in great demand'.[21]

The drought of 1933 was worsened by the international economic depression. By checking the expansion of European farming and hence the eviction of African tenants, the depression may have relieved some agrarian distress, but in other ways it accentuated it. The most important, as during the depression of 1922, was a collapse of cattle prices and a consequent increase in the relative price of grain. By the early 1930s African herds — numbering some 1 623 000 cattle in 1931 — may have been larger than at any time in the past, but there was little market for them. European ranchers, too, had built up their herds and, unable to export their relatively low-grade cattle to a remote and glutted world market, were often going out of business. A final blow came in 1931 when foot-and-mouth disease ended all exports, so that prices fell further.[22] During 1933 the selling price of a beast seldom rose above 20s. Often it was nearer to 15s., while in Belingwe the price of a cow fell at times to 7s. 6d.[23] Frequently there were no buyers. When the Native Commissioner in Ndanga arranged a cattle sale during June 1933, only three traders attended and paid between 15s. and 20s. for good oxen and 12s. 6d. for small cows, so that many beasts driven up to 190 km to the market were taken back unsold.[24] Some cattle owners refused to sell at the prices offered, but scarcity often left no choice. Whereas in the relatively good season of 1932 Africans had sold only 31 642 cattle, in 1933 they sold 81 081.[25]

Ironically, the depression probably did not reduce real wages. Money wages certainly fell substantially after 1927 when the 'tobacco rush' ended and European agriculture faltered. By 1933 farm wages were as low as six or seven shillings a month in some districts, or roughly half the levels of the mid-1920s. Yet because the depression also reduced food prices sharply, real wages probably maintained their value.[26] The problem of labour in 1933 was rather a shortage of work, for a temporary boom in gold-mining did not compensate for reductions in farm employment, so that many migrants made fruitless journeys in search of work.[27] Refusal to go out to work in time of famine — so much bewailed by officials before the First World War — disappeared from the records in 1933, to be replaced by occasional complaints that men 'blithely leave home when it suits them..... without regard to the welfare of the women and children.'[28] The capitalist economy was dominant.

This was even more clear in the operation of the grain market. Since the early colonial period, as European farmers produced an ever larger share of Southern Rhodesia's food, Africans needing grain had come to rely increasingly on purchases from European traders or on government relief. In 1928, for example, Europeans produced 62 per cent of Southern Rhodesia's maize and 84 per cent of the maize which was marketed; the equivalent figures in 1932 were 70 per cent and 89 per cent.[29] Meanwhile the export market for maize collapsed, the price falling from 11s. a bag early in 1930 to only 3s. 4d. in April 1931, far below the cost of production.[30] In response to the resulting European political pressure, the Government passed the Maize Marketing Act of 1931 which established a Maize Control Board to monopolize the purchase and sale of maize in Mashonaland. The Board bought maize at railhead depots at standard prices (6s. 6d. per bag in 1931/2). It sold as much as possible within Southern Rhodesia at fixed, relatively high prices (9s.2½. per bag). It then sold the surplus on the export market at low prices (5s. 4d. per bag.) The object was to distribute export losses to all maize growers in the controlled area.[31]

This system had several important effects on the dearth of 1933. First, it dramatically reduced the price which Africans obtained for grain sold to Europeans, especially in Mashonaland. Although the Maize Control Act allowed Africans within the controlled area to sell to the Board at standard prices if they delivered maize to railhead depots, few Africans could do this because nearly all Native Reserves were more than 40 km from a railway. Instead, African growers had to sell to European traders and farmers licensed by the Board as buying agents. This reduced competition among traders, the bargaining power of Africans, and the prices they obtained, especially in distant areas. In 1931 and 1932 Africans in remote parts of Mashonaland often received only 2s. or 2s. 6d. a bag for maize — sometimes paid in trade goods rather than cash — as against 7s. 6d. in regions which were not controlled.[32] By 1933 amendments had improved the situation a little, but producer prices remained very low even in a year of shortage. Nowhere in Mashonaland do they appear to have risen above 6s. a bag, while 4s. or less was sometimes quoted. In Lomagundi District there was still difficulty in selling grain for cash.[33]

A second effect of the new marketing system was to stabilize internal prices at relatively high levels. Whereas in earlier famines wholesale maize prices had fluctuated considerably during the season, in 1933 Salisbury prices varied only between a minimum of 9s. 6d. early in the year and a maximum of 11s. 6d. at its end.[34] Both prices were substantially higher than would have ruled in a free market. Prices in the districts probably did not rise to the very high levels seen in earlier famines, but 15s. or 17s. a bag was asked in some areas.[35] Much of the grain sold back to Africans had been bought directly from them, but the Control Board profited from the scarcity by selling a larger proportion of its grain than usual internally, where prices were 4s. a bag higher than in export markets. Whereas in 1932 the Board had exported 1 301 561 bags of maize, in 1933 it exported only 225 000 bags. It had large stocks, so that no grain was imported during 1933[36]

Not only did scarcity make the Control Board more effective than before, but it profited the European traders who were its local agents. Africans in general were becoming increasingly dependent on grain purchased from Europeans as the better African lands were over-used and growing numbers moved into arid sections of the Reserves. The government sought to check this decline by 'centralization', or planned farming and conservation in the Reserves, but this began only in 1929 and was still experimental.[37] In the meantime, although African cultivation was still expanding in favoured areas with vacant land, as a whole it was becoming a less effective defence against scarcity. Cassava, introduced with such optimism in 1922, had not won acceptance. Nor had local storage systems improved, except perhaps in Bikita District. Instead, the dependence on purchases from European traders was clear. 'As is usual, in a year of great shortage', wrote the Native Commissioner in Ndanga, 'the Trader and store-keeper must have done exceptionally good business and grain that had been traded in a previous year at a price of 5/- a bag in trade goods, roughly worth about 3/9 in cash, was valued and sold during the last month of the year at about 17/- for cash or cattle'.[38] As in 1922, many Native Commissioners reported Africans selling grain at low prices after harvest and buying it back at famine prices later in the season, presumably owing to immediate need for cash. Perhaps for the first time in Southern Rhodesia, the Native Commissioner in Mrewa reported a crop-lien system similar to those common in grain-growing areas of West Africa:

> The credit system would appear to be on the increase. The older men complain that the women and younger men pledge their growing crops for goods at the stores, and this to their mind has as much effect on the fixing of the season's price they receive, as the question of the supply and the demand. There is always uncertainty as to the ultimate yield of crops in any season, and to pledge even a small amount of grain to European traders, is a dangerous and objectionable practice which is difficult to control.[39]

Just as Africans relied heavily on White traders in 1933, so did the government. It had always sought to leave famine relief to private enterprise wherever possible, but in 1912, 1916, and 1922 the authorities had in practice taken the function increasingly into their hands. Now the trend was reversed. The Chief Native Commissioner's description of government relief in 1933 needs to be compared with the £72 302 which it had spent in 1922:

> The scarcity of food resulting from the poor crop, was met by encouraging traders to provide grain, a condition being that prices

were to be kept within reason, otherwise the department would intervene and provide grain at market rates. This resulted in traders supplying the bulk of the grain required, and in no instance was the intervention of the department necessary. In a few places, notably in the Melsetter district, where traders were either unable or unwilling to provide grain, and in cases of destitution, grain was supplied by the department, at cost price or on credit according to the circumstances of each case. The arrangements detailed above kept Government expenditure on relief down to a comparatively small sum. The total expended to the end of the year being approximately £900. The policy followed in this matter was dictated by the spirit of improvidence which had become manifest amongst the natives, amongst whom the saying had become common: 'Why worry? The government will feed us'.[40]

There were several reasons for the near-disappearance of government relief in 1933, except in Melsetter. One was that the scarcity itself was less severe than that of 1922, to say nothing of the crisis in Ndanga in 1916. A second reason was that the Maize Control Board, its grain stocks, and its licensed agents provided a distribution machinery which largely replaced that of the Native Affairs Department. Thirdly, the relief strategy of 1916 and 1922 had been Taylor's strategy, but he had retired in 1927 and his eventual successor, C.L. Carbutt, returned to the *laissez-faire* policy which Milton had favoured, partly from conviction, as his actions in earlier famines and his description of government relief suggest, and perhaps partly because he was under greater control by settler politicians now that Southern Rhodesia was internally self-governing. Relief works like road-building, pioneered in 1922, received little attention in 1933 from Native Commissioners and less from Africans. The government already required Africans to make and maintain roads without wages or rations even in good years.[41]

The fourth reason for the decline of government relief was precisely that the transport system had improved between 1922 and 1933 and could be left to distribute food by its normal operation. The chief innovation was motor transport. It is true that most rural transport and farm operations continued to rely on animal power until the Second World War. It is true, also, that reports on the scarcity of 1933 seldom mention motor transport. But the striking thing is that they never mention the problem of moving food by animal transport at the end of the dry season and during the rains, which had been the great difficulty in earlier famines. In 1933 Southern Rhodesia was thought to possess between 1 800 and 2 000 motor lorries, in addition to 11 400-12 500 motor cars. The most important motor transport service had been set up by the railway company in 1927; two years later it operated on fifteen routes feeding the railway network and an official noted that motor transport was permitting settlers in remote areas to enter commercial grain production.[42] The other transport innovation was a greater use of wheeled vehicles by Africans. In 1932 they owned 29 motor lorries, 68 motor cars, and 880 four-wheeled and 922 two-wheeled freight vehicles drawn by animals. In Mazoe District Africans had taken over the transport of grain from European farms to the railway.[43] When Chiefs from the remote Sabi valley warned Nielsen of their need for grain in June 1933, he 'told them that if they would bestir themselves they would probably find a European motor-lorry owner in the Village who would be willing to carry the grain to their areas at a modest rate'.[44]

In 1922 some scores of people had died during famine, chiefly in areas remote from transport. In 1933 there is no clear evidence that anyone died directly from famine, for two or three deaths from marasmus in February came so early in the year that it is difficult to attribute them to the famine.[45] A few smallpox cases occurred in several areas, causing six deaths in Inyanga District on the Portuguese border. The most serious epidemics of the year were whooping-cough in Umtali, which killed 133 children, and dysentery in Mrewa, which claimed 20 child victims during January, but neither was clearly related to the scarcity.[46] This, it appears, was not a famine that killed.

Instead, 1933 displayed a new pattern of scarcity, a pattern appropriate to a colony firmly dominated by European capitalism. Instead of acute famine concentrated in the most remote regions, Southern Rhodesia experienced a widespread and lingering scarcity which was serious both in isolated regions like the Sabi valley and in areas of intense European pressure like Matabeleland. This scarcity was a symptom not only of drought but of long-term decline in African grain production per head and short-term market fluctuations which depressed the price of cattle as against grain. Yet although Africans were becoming less capable of surviving famine by their own resources, scarcity was less likely to cause deaths because the European economy had acquired greater capacity to relieve distress, thanks to surplus grain production, controlled marketing and better transport. A capitalist system of famine control had to a critical extent supplanted the indigenous system of the past. More important, the new system was capable of continuing to control famine mortality despite African demographic growth and agricultural decline.

# CHAPTER 9

## War and Scarcity, 1942

The middle years of the Second World War[1] saw famine in many parts of tropical Africa, as more notoriously in India, where perhaps 3 500 000 died in the Bengal famine of 1943-4. The worst-affected country in Africa was Ruanda, where 300 000 people are alleged to have perished. Large areas of French West Africa also suffered extreme scarcity, as to a lesser extent did Northern Nigeria and arid regions of East Africa. Most of these African famines were precipitated by drought, but some were not, especially in Northern Nigeria, and almost all were more serious than the quality of the rains dictated. This was because they were worsened by wartime requisitions of food and labour and by a weakening of the mechanisms by which colonial governments had come to control famine mortality. As an official in French West Africa put it, 'the dearth of lorries put us back into the age which preceded the era of roads'. In parts of Northern Nigeria the famine of 1942-3 is remembered as a man-made, artificial scarcity. The same was true, more terribly, in Bengal, where the government's ill-judged intervention in the grain market created an entirely unnecessary famine.[2]

Southern Rhodesia did not at this time experience famine to compare with those in Ruanda or even French West Africa, but the scarcity which it suffered in 1942 bore much resemblance to them. It was precipitated by drought, but only localized drought which men would normally have survived without difficulty. Times were not normal, however, and scarcity was worsened by wartime distortions, especially distortions in the grain market. Yet other wartime circumstances minimized the scarcity, for Southern Rhodesia probably profited more and suffered less from the Second World War than any other country in the world. In the larger context, the important point about the scarcity of 1942 is that it continued and accentuated the patterns of change already seen in 1922 and 1933. More clearly than before, this was a capitalist scarcity relieved by capitalist means.

The years between 1934 and 1940 had been only moderately favourable for agriculture. Salisbury and Bulawayo registered less than average rainfall in three of those seven seasons, Fort Victoria in six out of seven. There was famine in the Sabi valley in 1934 and in arid areas of Sebungwe District in 1935, while in both those years many cattle died of poverty in Gwanda District. The southern and eastern lowveld suffered again in 1938. With these exceptions, however, the period passed without major crisis. In 1941, on the other hand, crops were poor in many districts despite reasonable rainfall everywhere save the Sabi valley, where less than 200 mm fell. Relief grain was needed there, in Gwanda District and the Gwaai Reserve in Matabeleland, and in the Nuanetsi area of southern Mashonaland. Little maize was exported during 1941. Fearing that stocks might not meet future demand, the authorities began to import grain from South Africa during July, for the first time for many years. In November, when even South African stocks ran low, orders were placed in Kenya and the Belgian Congo.[3] The year ended ominously with poor rains and a lack of reserves in Matabeleland, empty grain bins in the Zambezi valley, and 'indications of a general shortage of maize throughout the territory'.[4]

The scarcity worsened during 1942 as a second harvest failed in vulnerable regions. The most serious famine was in the middle Zambezi valley. Fifteen years later Dr Scudder suggested that during the 1940s this area may have experienced a crisis when land near the river could no longer support an increased population but bush fields were not yet common enough to supply the deficit.[5] However this may be, the valley suffered repeated famine at this time. Food was already scarce there early in 1942, when people were living on wild produce. The rain-fed harvest of 1942 failed completely and the annual flood must presumably also have been poor, for the relief grain needed in June had to be supplied sporadically for the rest of the year. By December scarcity was seriously affecting health. No deaths from hunger were reported, however, and early in the new year excellent rains ended the shortage, although a Native Commissioner thought that its physical effects on the aged and infirm were still visible at the end of 1943.[6]

By contrast, Mashonaland had a relatively good year during 1942. In the south, rainfall at Fort Victoria was 93 per cent of the average, famine relief ended even in the Sabi valley during March, late rains caused the cut finger millet to sprout again for a second crop, and food supplies were adequate throughout the year. The rest of Mashonaland had a similarly moderate year. Salisbury's rainfall was 89 per cent of normal. Crops in its immediate vicinity were excellent, but in the major maize-producing areas of Mazoe and Makoni Districts they were only enough for local needs, while there were shortages towards the end of the year in low-lying sections of Inyanga, Mrewa, and Hartley Districts. 'One child died indirectly due to shortage of grain food' in Hartley.[7] The absence of famine in Mount Darwin District, despite only 80 per cent of normal rainfall at district headquarters and the vagaries of the Zambezi flood, was especially striking and probably resulted from labour migration and the opening of the region to motor transport, which had attracted immigrants from elsewhere in Mashonaland and encouraged the highland areas of the district to produce important grain surpluses.

As was now normal, the widespread, nagging scarcity of 1942 centred in Matabeleland. Food relief was already being supplied there at the beginning of the year, especially in the arid Gwaai Reserve. But relief grain was scarce. 'Just sufficient coming in to keep them alive', the Native Commissioner in Gwanda reported in February,[8] while his colleague responsible for the severely-overcrowded Reserves of Matopo District complained that drought,

> coming on top of last years shortage of crops, has made the position desperate on account of the shortage of maize in the country ... Making allowance for natives at work, on a ration of 1 lb. per adult and 1/2 lb. per child the requirements of the district will be something like 100 bags per diem. The present amount released is nowhere near adequate.[9]

Meanwhile the crops of 1942 were withering in the fields. Rainfall was poor. Bulawayo received 74 per cent of its average and Hope Fountain only 57 per cent. The rain fell, moreover, on an agricultural system now concentrated on poor land and incapable of supporting the population even in normal years. By the middle of 1942 most districts were temporarily supplying their own needs from small harvests, but the situation worsened again in September. 'Practically every store in this District is thronged with natives buying grain', the Native Commissioner wrote from Matopo in October.[10] Two months later the crisis was more urgent. 'Natives are again storming into Trading Stores for meal supplies', Gwanda's Native Commissioner reported.[12] The rains were still poor in many parts of Matabeleland, but by February 1943 they were falling copiously and — in contrast to so much of tropical Africa — the harvest of 1943 was in some districts 'the most bountiful for many years'.[13]

Survival during 1942 owed much to the positive consequences of the war. In contrast to the situation in 1922 and 1933, there was in 1942 a lively demand for African cattle at a time when meat was scarce throughout the world. Prices had begun to move up in the late 1930s as the depression eased, but they accelerated on the outbreak of war. In contrast to the famine price of £1 per beast in 1933, prices in 1942 ranged between £3 and £5 per head and tended to rise through the year, averaging £3. 3s. 4d. in Gwanda in February 1942 and £4. 9s. 2d. in November.[14] African herds — 1 768 690 beasts in 1941 — were close to their peak levels and the government had in 1938 begun cautious destocking, so that sales were vigorously encouraged.[15] From this moment, especially in Matabeleland, cattle sales became the chief defence against famine.[16]

The war also created a strong demand for labour. Between 1933 and 1942 the number of African men in employment increased from 176 500 to 295 300. The proportion of these who were indigenous to Southern Rhodesia also rose from 42 to 46 per cent. In 1942 some 45 per cent of male taxpayers were in employment.[17] In the absence of cost of living statistics during the war, real wages cannot be calculated. They had risen in the late 1930s but were probably falling again as a result of wartime inflation. In 1946 they would be lower than at any time since 1934.[18] Several thousand men were conscripted for food production in 1942, which probably encouraged others to seek work independently.[19] In contrast to 1922 and 1933 there were no complaints that work-seekers could not find jobs and only one suggestion, from the Zambezi valley, that men preferred to stay and care for their families. Wage labour was becoming an ever more important defence against scarcity.

Conscription of labour to grow food was one indication that the complicated production and marketing structure created during the 1930s had run into difficulties. The Maize Control Act of 1931 had been amended in 1934 to extend control to the whole colony, harmonizing European interests at the expense of African producers.[20] The Maize Control Amendment Act of 1934 created two categories of maize, higher-priced 'local pool' maize and lower-priced 'export pool' maize, and laid down the proportion of his crop which each producer must contribute to each pool. (The two pools were entirely notional, for 'export pool' maize was not necessarily exported.) Africans who supplied maize to Control Board depots at railhead could supply to the local pool the same proportion of their crop as the average proportion supplied by all Europeans. African maize sold to traders, by contrast, was all initially regarded as export pool maize and rewarded at the lower rate, although none of it was actually exported. From 1935 a further amendment allowed 25 per cent of this maize to earn local pool prices. The proportion of African maize delivered direct to depots did not exceed 5 per cent during the 1930s and was deliberately reduced by the Board to almost nothing by 1939. Thereafter African producers received only the lower rate for the bulk of their maize, less the trader's transport costs and profits. In the later 1930s they sold to traders at between 2s. and 6s. a bag,[21] although many traded among themselves at higher prices. In Bubi district in 1940, for example, the official producer price was 4s. 6d. a bag but Africans preferred to deal among themselves at 8s. to 10s. a bag.[22]

This marketing system had complicated effects on African agriculture. Total grain output increased and a larger proportion was marketed, in order to maintain incomes despite falling prices. Maize continued to replace millet as the staple food of most Shona, especially on the better-watered land nearest roads and railways. The result was increasing pressure on land in the Reserves, whose population rose between 1933 and 1941 from 675 499 to 854 746, owing to a natural increase of nearly 3 per cent a year and continued evictions from European estates.[23] Average yields may well have fallen as more marginal land was cultivated; one estimate suggested that between 1900 and 1950 African cultivated acreage increased by 260-270 per cent but grain output by only 140 per cent.[24] Certainly the Government's alarm was shown by decisions in 1936 to emphasize soil conservation and in 1938 to begin destocking, although between 1939 and 1945 less than 3 per cent of agricultural development expenditure was directed to Africans.[25] Meanwhile the very low prices obtained for grain in districts remote from transport may have reduced cultivation there and led many Africans to prefer wage labour. Average grain output per head of the African population continued to decline, from 2,87 bags in 1929-33 to 2,68 in 1934-8 and 2,44 in 1938-42.[26] This long-term decline in African production helps to explain why severe scarcity occurred in 1942 despite the fact that the average harvest was only marginally below the norm for the period: 2,22 bags per head in 1941 and 2,35 in 1942.[27] European farms, which regularly provided over 70 per cent of marketed maize, had very poor crops in both years. In 1939/40 Europeans delivered 1 059 000 bags to the Maize Marketing Board; in 1940/1, 682 000; in 1941/2, 686 000.[28]

The hunt for foreign grain which had begun in July 1941 became frantic in the early months of 1942. Kenya declared that it could not supply a promised 100 000 bags. South Africa was short of grain but undertook to send what it could, although at a price 50 per cent higher than six months earlier. In the Americas surplus maize was being burned as fuel, but shipping was unobtainable during wartime. Supplies were finally procured from Argentina, but at nearly twice the price which South Africa had charged in 1941. Altogether, 495 000 bags of grain were imported during 1941/2.[29] In January 1942 the Maize Control Board had to issue quotas to shopkeepers and instruct them to limit each customer to 25 lb. at a time. Labour rations were reduced by 25 per cent in February, provoking a scattering of strikes.[30] The quantities then reaching districts like Bulawayo and Matopo which relied heavily on marketed maize were quite inadequate to feed the population. 'The next two months will be a very anxious time indeed', warned the Native Commissioner in Bulawayo.[31] By May, however, the new harvest was relieving pressure on the Control Board's supplies. When demand began to increase again in August, European deliveries to the Board and imports from South Africa ensured that there was sufficient grain in the stores. Occasional local shortages were reported thereafter, but generally a ration of 1½ lb.

a day per man, 1 lb. per woman, and ½ lb. per child was available. Prices were tightly controlled and were allowed to rise only about one shilling a bag during the year.[32] Traders outside the cities could add only their true costs. Africans with surplus grain continued to trade amongst themselves at rates close to official retail prices.

The most striking point about grain distribution during 1942 was its complete control by the Maize Control Board and its storekeeper-agents. In Matopo or Gwanda it was the stores that were 'thronged' or 'stormed', not a Native Commissioner's relief depot as at Bikita in 1916. Moreover, almost all grain was sold for cash, thanks to the relatively high prices of cattle and the availability of work. The government supervised the Board, of course, but the depleted district staff — nearly half the personnel of the Native Affairs Department were on active service — concentrated on checking storekeepers' prices and arranging free issues to 'old men, women and children' and the incapacitated.[33] Relief works were not mentioned in the labour-hungry Southern Rhodesia of 1942. All this was in accordance with the rules for famine relief which Chief Native Commissioner Carbutt had issued in May 1941 when scarcity had first appeared likely. 'The Government', he had announced in familiar terms, 'prefers not to interfere with private enterprise, and therefore whenever possible the grain requirements of Natives should be supplied by local store-keepers', although Native Commissioners must 'insist on profits being kept within reasonable bounds'. Only if the stores could not cope should the authorities intervene directly, issuing one pound of grain per head per day, preferably whole maize because the effort of preparing it would cause recipients to be economical. Free issues should be made only to the absolutely indigent. 'While it is not desired that anyone should die of hunger', Carbutt had explained, 'the greatest care has to be exercised to prevent people, who are not in real want, drawing food supplies merely because they are easily obtained.' Instead, food must be paid for in cash, cattle (the payer herding the stock until needed), or credit, 'provided that some person with a fixed address holds himself responsible for payment within twelve months of receiving the grain'.[34] The principle of relying on the commercial structure to relieve scarcity was more fully observed in 1942 than ever before, but only because the Maize Control Board had taken charge of food distribution throughout the colony.

The only reported death convincingly attributable to the scarcity of 1942 was the child who 'died indirectly due to shortage of grain food' in Hartley District in December.[35] In that month other districts reported three deaths from marasmus (Gwelo and Salisbury), one from pellagra (Matopo), eight from scurvy (Bubi and Bulawayo), and three from malnutrition (Concession and Chipinga).[36] None of these was explicitly attributed to the scarcity, but it may have caused or contributed to some of them and of the many other deficiency diseases which no doubt went unreported. There was no epidemic disease in 1942. This was a scarcity of the new kind, not a famine of the old.

# CHAPTER 10

## Peace and Scarcity, 1947

The drought of 1947 displayed in extreme form the new pattern of scarcity and the new methods of countering it.[1] Potentially, 1947 was a very severe crisis. The drought and harvest failure were the worst of the colonial period. They took place when food stocks were already low. They created serious scarcity in Southern Rhodesia's two danger points: the Zambezi valley, where an old pattern of famine survived, and Matabeleland, where a new pattern had resulted from colonial change. In Matabeleland, especially, the drought of 1947 interacted with a deepening crisis in African agriculture. It was met, moreover, by an even more complete reliance than before on the new capitalist pattern of famine relief, centring on territorial control of grain supplies, distribution through private traders, and cash purchases. Finally, there were indications of that endemic malnutrition among the poor which was replacing famine mortality as the chief problem of subsistence.

The drought came when food was already scarce. Following the shortage in 1943, the harvest of 1944 was good, but in 1945 crops failed widely in Matabeleland and maize meal was again rationed. This was repeated in 1946: Mashonaland had a fair harvest but Matabeleland suffered another shortage and depended on purchased grain at the end of the year. By then drought threatened the whole colony and the authorities sought permission from London to import 300 000 bags of grain.[2] The rains of 1946/7 were even worse than had been feared. By 4 April, Bulawayo and Fort Victoria had each received only 33 per cent of their normal rainfall and Salisbury 54 per cent, all of these figures being the lowest since records began. The resulting harvest was disastrous not only for Africans but for the European farmers whose grain was essential to African subsistence. Whereas in the poor 1945/6 season Europeans had supplied 795 000 bags of maize to the Control Board and Africans 302 000, in the dreadful 1946/7 season they supplied only 394 000 and 203 000 bags respectively — the lowest annual total during the thirty years after the Board's formation in 1931. There was scarcity in all but six of the colony's thirty-six Districts.[3]

This short-term crisis interacted with Southern Rhodesia's long-term agrarian problem. By 1943, 13,2 million of the colony's 38,9 million ha had been alienated to Europeans.[4] Another 6,4 million ha were set aside for future alienation, 0,4 million were forest reserves, and 7,2 million had not yet been allocated to either race. This left 11,7 million ha for

Africans: 8,6 million as native reserves and 3,2 million as Native Purchase Areas where progressive African farmers could buy quasi-freehold farms — by 1947 only 2 192 of these had been demarcated, covering 199 314 ha.[5] Some Native Reserves in Mashonaland were on the highveld, especially in the north, but more were in the less-favoured middleveld and lowveld. This pattern was more clearly marked in Matabeleland, where only a few patches of highveld remained in African hands. In the early years of European settlement the effects of alienation had been muted by the sparsity of the population and the willingness of European landowners to allow Africans to remain on their otherwise unused estates in return for rent in cash or labour. By the late 1940s, however, the real effects of land alienation were becoming clear. The African population had increased by 1946 to perhaps 2 270 000 and was growing at over 3 per cent each year.[6] The number of Africans living on White-owned land remained fairly stable at about 150 000-160 000.[7] Most of the remainder crowded ever more densely into the Reserves, whose population rose between 1941 and 1948 from 854 746 to 1 174 890.[8]

The eviction of unwanted Africans from European land was especially marked after the Second World War. The war itself had brought real prosperity to European farming for the first time. Between 1939 and 1946, for example, the price of Rhodesian flue-cured tobacco rose from 10,11d. to 32,37d. per pound.[9] The gross output of European agriculture was to multiply twenty times between 1944 and 1976.[10] Part of the expansion was due to an influx of 'soldier settlers'; Southern Rhodesia's White population grew between 1946 and 1960 from 82 386 to 223 000.[11] Part resulted from the mechanization of agriculture, which began seriously at this time. Part was due to the cultivation of land hitherto left for African use, especially sandy soils in Mashonaland which were ideal for tobacco. In Makoni District, for example, Professor Ranger has shown that loss of land in the 1940s was far more bitterly resented than in the 1890s, for now there was no alternative good land for Africans to use. Between 1933 and 1947 the population of the Native Reserves in Makoni District rose from 27 243 to 49 556.[12] 'In many districts the problem of placing persons displaced from the European area is becoming acute', the Chief Native Commissioner reported in 1946.[13] During 1947 the government bought 170 000 ha of alienated land for temporary occupation by evicted Africans.[14]

When serious land scarcity first became apparent during the 1930s, the government adopted a policy called 'centralization' which demarcated arable and pastoral regions in each Reserve, so that land could be used more efficiently, and encouraged soil conservation and improved husbandry, all in the hope of enabling larger numbers to subsist on a fixed quantity of land — although in practice these provisions may have worsened the situation in bad years by preventing the exploitation of vleis and other fragile resources.[15] During the 1940s, as pressure continued to grow, emphasis switched to destocking, which halved the excess stock in 34 overstocked Reserves between 1945 and 1947.[16] But it was clear by 1947 that destocking was no solution. The Reserves had too many people rather than too many cattle. If the people were to manure their land, they needed more cattle rather than fewer. Already officials were contemplating the measures to reduce the rural population which took shape in the Land Husbandry Act of 1951.[17] In the meantime, studies of agriculture in the Reserves suggested ever lower yields per ha, while African grain production per head continued to decline.[18]

Against this background, the harvest of 1947 followed a now familiar pattern. In northern and central Mashonaland the crops were patchy. In Mazoe District, with the best maize land in the colony, Africans sold 45 340 bags of maize during 1947 as against 47 904 during the previous year,[19] but in Hartley District small quantities of famine relief were necessary. Overpopulated but well-watered Manicaland had relatively good harvests. The worst-affected areas of Mashonaland were once-prosperous Gutu and Chilimanzi Districts, whose inhabitants had gradually been crowded into ill-watered Reserves. Chilimanzi's Reserves supported 18 036 people in 1933 and 31 061 in 1947; its African inhabitants produced only 2 000 bags of maize in 1947 as against 23 000 in 1945.[20] Gutu's Reserves — with 38 083 people in 1933 and 60 650 in 1947 — had been the target of the colony's most ruthless destocking, losing three-eighths of their livestock between 1945 and 1947.[21] In 1945/6 the eastern half of the District had only 130 mm of rain and no reserves to carry forward. When the rains failed again early in 1947 — varying from 380 to less than 100 mm — Gutu suffered its worst drought in human memory. 'Natives in anticipating certain famine are already pressing for relaxation of destocking', the Native Commissioner reported in February, 'as they want to eat their cattle rather than have to sell them and receive money which they cannot eat.'[22] Chibi District, further south, also had low reserves and experienced a disastrous harvest, with only 200 mm of rain at district headquarters. It relied on imported grain throughout the year. Bikita, too, had one of the worst years in living memory and crops failed in parts of Fort Victoria, Ndanga, and especially Nuanetsi, where two-thirds of the population had no crops, some famine foods failed, and people travelled 30 km to fetch domestic water.[23] The Sabi valley, by contrast, needed little relief, partly owing to irrigation schemes which now covered over 800 ha.[24] Even more striking was the advance made in Mount Darwin District, now an important focus of immigration and development. Although crops failed in parts of the District, others had surpluses and a network of African traders ensured that no relief was needed in this formerly famine-prone District.[25]

The contrast with conditions further up the Zambezi valley was striking. This was the most backward part of Southern Rhodesia and an ancient pattern of famine survived:

> The Zambesi Valley natives have fared badly with almost total crop failures due to negligible rains. When they realised that their main crops had failed they abandoned their kraals and moved to the Zambesi River to establish Winter maize lands. The Zambesi rose several feet in April, in consequence of copious rains in Barotseland, and many promising maize gardens were flooded. Yet a third planting was made possible by distributing maize seed, their own having been exhausted. Elephant proved such a nuisance that gardens had to be made on the islands — even then elephant were known to swim across and raid. A severe frost eventually damaged the maize and so every diligent effort to produce crops failed.
>
> These lowveld dwellers, hardened as they are to not infrequent famines, were forced to subsist on hunger-diet — whatever they could find in the bush such as roots and tree beans.[26]

Here alone, it appears, famine may have been directly responsible for deaths. 'Malnutrition was very apparent on the Zambesi', the Native Commissioner in Sebungwe wrote, 'and there four cases of death from actual starvation (were) reported. Unfortunately it was impossible to prove or disprove whether the cause of death was actual starvation or whether lack of food was merely a contributory cause.'[27]

Matabeleland did not report deaths from starvation, but its crop failure was at least as serious. In Belingwe District, where only 190 mm of rain fell, no maize and only one-quarter of the normal crop of small grain was reaped. In Gwanda crops failed completely for the second successive season. 'There has been an acute shortage of food supplies throughout the year', the Native Commissioner reported, 'and at one stage the position became critical and many natives were very close to starvation'. He added, however, that only some 10 per cent of cattle had died from poverty,[28] a point echoed in other Districts which had sometimes lost half or more of their stock in previous droughts. This was attributed in part to destocking. Yet harvest failure was almost universal in Matabeleland and the people depended on the trading system until they, together with the rest of the colony, could reap the wonderful crops of 1948 which ended the famine.

Because the government foresaw scarcity late in 1946, it made preparations well in advance, utilizing the skill in famine relief accumulated over half a century. Because London had still not authorized imports and there must be delay before they could arrive, maize rationing was announced in January 1947, the cultivation of quick-growing crops was ordered, Native Commissioners were required to estimate relief needs, and meetings were held throughout the country to warn Africans of the danger. These precautions created a degree of panic. 'An immediate and direct result of notifying Natives of the shortage of maize in the Colony', one Native Commissioner reported, 'was to increase tenfold the demand for meal at the local stores'.[29] Many store-keepers had difficulty in obtaining supplies from millers. In mid-February the Chief Native Commissioner recommended the importation of 600 000 bags of grain, partly from Argentina.[30] By April the arrangements were made, grain began to arrive, and rationing was lifted. Then the grain ships were delayed, the colony was left with only seven days' supply, and only frantic appeals to South Africa brought relief. Not until September was the flow of grain assured.[31] In all, Africans bought 500 000 bags of grain during the year and would have bought more if available — Gutu received only half the grain it sought.[32] The Maize Control Board handled most of the grain, transporting it by rail and lorry to storekeepers for distribution. No free issues were made and credit issues totalled less than £1 000, nearly all in Gutu District, where the Native Commissioner answered criticisms by explaining that he had given credit to only 10 per cent of applicants: 310 widows, 105 grass widows, 42 cripples and defectives, 265 old and infirm, 18 blind, and their 1 217 children. He eventually recovered over 90 per cent of the money.[33] This is the first time in the Colony's history', the Chief Native Commissioner claimed, 'that we have had a major drought and famine which has cost the Government practically nothing by way of famine relief to the Native population'. Twenty-five years earlier, he added, 'Famine Relief in drought years was common and cost thousands of pounds'.[34]

The distribution system relied on private traders. In towns these were often Indians, while African storekeepers controlled trade in remote Districts like Mount Darwin, but in rural areas European traders generally had the largest share of business. 'The necessity of having a few good European Stores in a Reserve of this size have (sic) been proved during the past year', the Native Commissioner in Belingwe reported. 'European storekeepers were the only ones capable of undertaking the supply of maize and meal and without them this Department would have been faced with the problem of supplying the whole of the Reserve.'[35] The government generally confined itself to enforcing price controls. The producer price of maize to European farmers in 1946/7 was 25s. a bag. The official consumer price was 20s., which rose to 30s. when transport costs to remote areas were added. Higher prices ruled in uncontrolled trade among Africans.[36] Only rarely did the government have to provide grain, as in Gwanda District during July and August when three truckloads of maize distributed by the authorities averted threatening starvation.[37] The proliferation of motor vehicles during and after the war facilitated transport, even into the remote Zambezi valley. There, in addition, 'herds of pack donkeys can be seen returning from the railhead loaded with what grain the owners have been able to purchase',[38] and animal transport remained essential in many regions. Sometimes even this was inadequate. In Chibi District, for example, unavoidable delays occurred in the transport of food supplies and actual hunger was suffered by those in native villages. Natives had to walk considerable distances on frequent occasions to get small quantities of food and sometimes were disappointed and returned home empty handed.'[39] Crowds are reported to have camped around rural stores until they could obtain enough grain to carry home.[40]

Almost all this grain was bought for cash, at a cost of approximately £750 000.[41] Even impoverished areas like the Zambezi valley found the necessary money. Most cash came from the sale of 202 815 cattle, as against 161 671 in 1946. Average prices remained at their wartime level of over £4 per beast, thanks to post-war economic expansion and the establishment of authorized markets. Total receipts were estimated at £862 000.[42] The other main source of cash was wage-labour. The number of indigenous African men employed rose between 1942 and 1947 from 134 000 to 183 000, the latter figure representing 47,5 per cent of all such men.[43] Several Districts reported, without apparent alarm, that 70 per cent of their men were away in employment. As the Provincial Native Commissioner in Matabeleland put it, 'The policy was that superfluous natives should leave kraals and work for their living'.[44] There was no lack of jobs and no relief works were organized. Real wages, on the other hand, were very low as a result of inflation which augmented the cost of living for a single African by 144 per cent between August 1939 and August 1947.[45] In 1946 real agricultural wages were 28 per cent lower than in 1914, and there seems to have been little increase during 1947.[46] Labour tenants earning 10s. or 12s. a month suffered especially when maize meal rose to over 25s. a bag.[47] The families of migrant labourers could fare even worse: there were accounts of subsistence prostitution by women temporarily abandoned by husbands.[48] Yet at least one Native Commissioner stressed the continuing strength of family obligations. 'Pathetic cases have arisen', he wrote, 'where the responsibility of a man's family has proved too much for him and he has deserted them. Never are they allowed to starve as even distant relatives will rally round to support them.'[49]

Only the four deaths reported from the Zambezi valley were officially ascribed to starvation, although with much uncertainty. Others may have gone unknown or unreported. Two serious epidemics took place, but their relationship to food scarcity is not clear. Measles killed numerous children in Bikita District, and for the first time since 1922 dearth coincided with a smallpox epidemic, which caused 181 reported cases (with 1 death) in 1946, 685 cases (with 117 deaths) in 1947, 1 823 cases (with 425 deaths) in 1948, and 861 cases (with 60 deaths) in 1949. Most deaths were among Tonga in Wankie District who had hitherto avoided vaccination.[50] The authorities saw smallpox chiefly as a disease imported from neighbouring colonies rather than connected with food scarcity. They accepted, however, that the shortages of 1947 seriously damaged nutrition, and consequently general health, in many regions, especially among children.[51] Concern with nutrition had surfaced occasionally in Southern Rhodesia since the mid-1930s, but little had been done. In April 1947 a Nutrition Council was at last established, although without the powers or staff it wanted.[52] Two years later a small survey showed 22,9 per cent of African schoolchildren in the two lowest nutritional categories, as against 11,4 per cent of European schoolchildren.[53] Some feared that the colony faced a chronic shortage of food, but during the next decade it was the poor, rather than the population as a whole, who suffered from the new patterns of scarcity and relief.

# CHAPTER 11

## Prosperity and Scarcity, 1960

The 1950s were a prosperous decade for Southern Rhodesia, as for most of tropical Africa.[1] Climatically they were the best years since the 1870s. Between 1951/2 and 1958/9, Salisbury averaged 12 per cent more than its normal rainfall, Fort Victoria and Bulawayo 19 per cent more. African grain production per head, which had fallen to 2,18 bags a year between 1948 and 1953, rose again to 2,96 bags between 1953 and 1957, although it never regained the average of 3 bags or more normal before 1930.[2] The grain produced was increasingly maize, owing to higher world prices in the early 1950s, the spread of grinding mills, and consumer preferences. Between 1948/9 and 1959/60 the estimated area of African-grown maize rose from 266 500 to 500 000 ha, while that of millet and sorghum fell from 425 000 to 380 000 ha.[3] European maize deliveries to the Control Board rose from an average of 890 000 bags a year between 1948/9 and 1951/2 to 2 553 000 bags a year between 1955/6 and 1958/9,[4] although the main growth point of European farming at this time was tobacco.

At the end of the decade this prosperity was interrupted by serious scarcity. The harvest of 1958/9 was poor. That of 1959/60 was disastrous, chiefly owing to drought. While Salisbury received 86 per cent of its average rainfall in 1959/60, Fort Victoria enjoyed only 67 per cent and Bulawayo 55 per cent. As these figures suggest, the drought varied greatly in severity between regions. Its impact also depended on diverse agrarian conditions. Generally, however, the scarcity marked a new stage in the history of food shortage in Southern Rhodesia. This was still a capitalist dearth and it was relieved by capitalist means. But the grain trade was less dominant than in 1947. More people needed direct government relief, especially among the poor. Clinical evidence of malnutrition was more extensive than before. This is difficult evidence to interpret, but it appears that the prosperity of the 1950s, the further development of capitalism, and certain official policies had marked out more clearly a category of marginal people who were the chief sufferers during scarcity. The capitalist economy could not support these people or absorb the labour supply made available by land alienation and a rising population. In 1960 Southern Rhodesia's per capita Gross Domestic Product began to decline after many years of growth.[5] The scarcity of that year revealed that settler capitalism was entering a crisis which would produce a sequence of food shortages during the next 20 years, would provide the context for political liberation, and would continue with growing severity during the first years of African rule. That this pattern should have survived dramatic political change illustrates the close relationship between the structure of an economic system and the nature of scarcity within it.

\* \* \* \*

Even the maize-growing districts of northern and central Mashonaland felt the scarcity of 1960. In Mazoe District the old men of the Bushu Reserve complained of the worst season since the British occupation. Crops were less disastrous in Mazoe's other Reserves, but the steady growth of population — from 30 500 in 1947 to 37 092 in 1960 — was driving men to exploit ever more marginal land.[6] The Chiweshe Reserve, for example, was designed to support 2 500 people cultivating 8 000 ha and keeping 20 000 stock; in 1957 it actually supported 5 480 people cultivating 24 250 ha and keeping only 19 297 stock. The need for food made balanced farming impossible there. In 1960/1 maize occupied over 80 per cent of the Reserve's cultivated land. The average yield of 7,4 bags per ha was equal to that which Europeans reaped in sandy areas, but was only a quarter of their yields on heavier soils.[7] Most striking was that yields averaged 10,3 bags in those areas which the inadequate stock could manure, but only 4,7 bags on unmanured land.[8] 'Of every ten acres sown to maize in this particular season', a researcher wrote, 'no fewer than six produced no harvest ... Patches of first and second class crops thus stand out on the ... ground as islands in a barren waste.'[9] Makoni District also had poor crops in 1960. Since 1947 the inhabitants of its Reserves had increased from 49 556 to 77 675. 'The pressure on the land', wrote the Native Commissioner, 'is now very great indeed'.[10] Where population was less dense, highveld crops were better and scarcity was concentrated, as so often in the past, in the arid lowveld: the Pfungwe Reserve in Mrewa District, the southern Maranke Reserve in Umtali, and the arid lowveld of northern Inyanga. In Mount Darwin District, similarly, there was shortage in the Dande, but all necessary food was available from the higher Kandeya Reserve, which had developed during the previous twenty years into a major maize producer. Yet even in Kandeya the swollen population was spilling off the heavy red soils on to infertile land.[11]

This dual pattern of scarcity — in overpopulated as well as arid regions — was apparent elsewhere in Mashonaland in 1960. Gutu District had seen its Reserve population increase since 1947 from 60 650 to 110 122. 'One could not call it a drought year', the Native Commissioner wrote, 'but rainfall was poor and erratic and crops were poor'. He reported widespread malnutrition among infants and hardship among the aged and infirm.[12] Yet the worst scarcity in Mashonaland in 1960 was in the south. This time the focus was not the Sabi valley, where, thanks to some 1 600 ha of irrigation, crops were better than in the neighbouring highlands.[13] The main shortage was rather in Fort Victoria, Chibi, and Nuanetsi Districts on the southern border. Several of Fort Victoria's Reserves needed famine relief. Chibi reported 'scattered famine in most of the district' and children too weak to go to school.[14] In Nuanetsi the two sources of hunger came together and widespread crop failure was worsened by the opening of many new ranches on alienated land, whose owners often evicted African residents or sometimes employed them for as little as 10s. a month.[15]

One area of recurrent famine no longer troubled the authorities. In the Zambezi valley, where Tonga had so often hungered, the waters of Lake Kariba were rising over deserted villages. Yet Tonga still hungered. Resettled on the plateau south of the lake, and no longer able to supplement dryland fields with riverside gardens, they needed nearly 4 000 bags of famine relief in 1960.[16] Objectively, the Zambezi valley had been no paradise, but Tonga came to imagine it so. 'People claim that in the valley life was good, much better than it is today', Dr Weinrich found in 1974, 'that they always had plenty of food and that they were never hungry, that they had always clean water and that a large variety of wild fruit was always at hand.'[17]

By contrast, the other area of endemic famine, southern Matabeleland, was the chief victim of 1960. There was indeed scarcity throughout Matabeleland and also in the Gwelo region, which suffered its third successive poor harvest, but the only area north of Bulawayo to report extreme shortage was Nyamandhlovu, where one of the worst recorded droughts was intensified by the effects of land alienation:

> Owing to the severe drought in the sub-district during the last two years, many land owners have had to reduce their labour forces. This has resulted in many Africans being turned off private farms where they had lived and worked all their lives. In 20 such cases the men concerned were born on these properties. None of them can find employment in the sub-district or in the towns, neither can any place be found for them to live in the neighbouring districts or Forest Areas. The land owner in each case has been persuaded to allow them to remain, but this is only a temporary solution. With the advent of more intensive farming in the European area, the problem of these landless Africans is going to increase.[18]

South of Bulawayo, this combination of drought and land shortage was the norm in the lowveld, where the expansion of European ranching since the Second World War had left too little land to support the African inhabitants as pastoralists, obliging them to cultivate drought-prone regions suited only to herding.[19] Parts of Shabani District had only 100 mm of rain during 1960 and lost 95 per cent of their crops. Gwanda suffered complete harvest failure, sold 35 407 of its cattle, lost another 19 856 by death, and possessed only 50 266 at the end of the year. Close to Tuli on the South African border there were less than 250 mm of rain and a fifth successive harvest failure for 'people who prior to their removal to the area were accustomed to reap sufficient grain for their own use and a surplus for sale'.[20]

Overall, the pressure on land in African areas was now very acute. The African population continued to grow at over 3 per cent a year.[21] The total land allocated to them was 16,8 million ha. The population of this area increased between 1948 and 1961 from 1 401 411 to 2 321 338. The area allocated to Europeans was 19,2 million ha, including 86 per cent of the colony's best land. Only 3 per cent of European land was cultivated. During 1960 a committee chaired by the Minister of Native Affairs recommended that this apportionment of land must be abandoned.[22] It certainly underlay the prevailing scarcity. In contrast to 1942 or 1947, there was plenty of grain in Southern Rhodesia in 1960. At the beginning of the year the Grain Marketing Board had some three million bags of white maize in stock, and although deliveries during 1960 were the lowest since 1953, stocks at the end of the year were almost as large as at the beginning.[23] The problem was that Africans produced an exceptionally low proportion of their own needs: only 1,87 bags per head, as against an average of 2,84 bags during the previous five years.[24] Everything, therefore, depended on their capacity to buy in the market. This, in turn, rested more than ever on wage-employment. Since 1948 African real wages had increased by 34 per cent. The number of African men employed had risen since 1947 from 387 000 to 647 000.[25] After 1957, however, this growth slowed markedly.[26] Economic expansion no longer kept pace with population increase, given that land scarcity obliged almost all the increase to seek wage-employment. Concern with African unemployment emerged in the late 1950s.[27] During the drought of 1960 Africans seeking work often could not find it, a dilemma they had not faced since the scarcity of 1933. Early in 1960 an estimated 4 000-5 000 Africans were seeking work in Bulawayo, 43 per cent of whom came from drought-stricken areas.[28]

The other source of cash on which Africans relied during scarcity was their cattle. These again played a vital role. Despite over twenty years of sporadic destocking, total African herds — 1 953 000 beasts in 1960 — were almost as numerous as at any time in the twentieth century.[29] Some 236 535 were sold in 1960, as against 153 334 in 1958 and 152 177 in 1959.[30] The average price for fair average quality beasts, £19. 16s. 7d, was a record, although the average for all cattle was perhaps only two-thirds or three-quarters of this.[31] The increase in prices since 1947 roughly matched the rise in grain prices. Deaths of cattle from poverty during 1960, added to sales, severely depleted some district herds, as figures for Gwanda illustrate.[32] Yet cattle sales alone could not meet scarcity. An outbreak of foot-and-mouth disease interrupted sales in southern Matabeleland, while the rapid increase in the human population meant that each African owned on average fewer cattle than before: only 0,79 per head in 1960, as against 1,64 in 1931.[33] In practice, this meant that a growing number of rural households had no cattle at all. Studies made in the 1960s and 1970s suggested that one-third of families in the Reserves were without cattle.[34] The marginalization of the rural poor was encouraged by the Land Husbandry Act of 1951, which attempted to make the Reserves viable by reorganizing African farming practices, especially by giving cultivators a negotiable title to a consolidated plot of arable land, in theory 3,24 ha where land was of high quality. Although the Act was designed to check capitalist farming in the Reserves and to entrench a small peasantry, the fact that the Reserves contained only two-thirds of the necessary land meant that many families obtained sub-economic plots and responded by shedding their more marginal members, especially the old and the young. In one overpopulated Reserve area in Fort Victoria District studied during the mid-1960s, 81 per cent of the men aged less than 30 were landless.[35]

Where the settler capitalist economy could no longer provide relief from scarcity, many sought it in indigenous resources. Even in normal years most surplus grain produced by Africans was sold directly to neighbours, but in 1960 this form of exchange was especially important. In Gutu District, for example, 'There was tremendous sale of grains between areas where fair crops were reaped and areas where crops were particularly poor'.[36] The chief reason for by-passing traders was probably that they paid producers less but charged buyers more than the prices at which direct exchange took place. In Chiweshe Reserve in 1960-1 the Grain Marketing Board's selling price was two-and-one-half times its buying price.[37] Apart from exchange, the other indigenous resource was wild produce. This was widely exploited during 1960. 'While all areas are short of food now', the Native Commissioner in Nuanetsi reported, 'nature has come to their aid with the greatest hatching of mopani caterpillars experienced for years.'[38] 'One indication of the shortage of food' in

Bindura 'is the sight of parties setting out for the veld to collect fruits and edible roots. The "muzhanje" crop has been picked to the last wild loquat.'[39] Yet by 1960 capitalism had penetrated the bush. The wild fruits of Bindura were sold to lorry-owning traders from Salisbury at 1s. 6d. per bucket.[40]

Important as they were, indigenous resources could not make up for the fact that the strains within the capitalist economy left more people vulnerable to scarcity in 1960 than at any time since 1922. The result was a renewed reliance on government relief. The authorities preserved their long-standing reluctance to issue free rations. 'When food was made available for Africans', a junior minister explained in February, 'it was not a gift from the Government. The Africans had either to pay for the mealie meal and other food or work for it by employment on Government development work.'[41] Altogether some £28 000 was owed for food at the end of the year.[42] Much of it was owed in areas like the Gwaai Reserve where foot-and-mouth disease prevented cattle sales. Some grain was sold at subsidized prices, especially to the resettled Tonga. In Fort Victoria District famine relief was issued 'particularly to old widows and men incapable of working and those who have no stock — in order to prevent starvation.' Similar issues were made on credit to some 350 old or incapacitated people in Chibi District.[43] For the able-bodied, the authorities organized relief works on a scale not seen since 1922, when also wage-employment had been scarce. Some 1 500 were so employed in Belingwe District at the end of the year. Gangs in Fort Victoria District worked on soil conservation projects. In Shabani an average of 400-500 people constructed tank dams in return for food worth two shillings a day. 'The majority of those who work are women', the Native Commissioner reported, the men being unenthusiastic.[44]

Accounts of the scarcity of 1960 laid more stress on the special suffering of the poor and vulnerable than had been common in recent shortages. One cannot be sure that this signified a real departure, but there were indications that differentiation among Africans since the Second World War had left some at special risk. One indication came from Bulalima-Mangwe:

> More and more applications for assistance are coming in. Undoubtedly the drought caused considerable hardship, but the drought sufferers were able to obtain grain on credit from Native Affairs Department, repayment to be made when sales start again.
> The problem cases are the elderly and cripples. Under the Land Husbandry Act they find that those who supported them now have restricted land areas (they cannot plough where they wish), and it is probable that many of these applicants for assistance are

told to come in by relatives who can no longer look after them under the Land Husbandry individual holding system.[45]

Other Native Commissioners also felt that support for elderly and disabled kin had weakened. The expansion of European farming created similar problems. 'Several pathetic cases who had lived all their lives on European farms — only to be ordered off when they were unable from old age to render further service — came to notice', it was reported from Fort Victoria. 'Fortunately, however, pleas from this office to reconsider eviction appear to have succeeded.' Famine relief was needed there chiefly for old widows, the incapacitated and those lacking stock.[46] In Que Que District hardship was concentrated 'among the poorest agriculturalist'.[47]

The other group who suffered especially in 1960 were children. A few deaths from smallpox and 46 from measles were reported during the year, but nothing related these explicitly to food scarcity.[48] Its effects among children were seen rather in malnutrition, although the effects were difficult to identify in a colony where malnutrition was coming to be seen as the main endemic health problem.[49] Especially serious malnutrition was found among the children of those employed on famine relief works in Shabani District. Scarcity also bred malnutrition among children in the Gwaai Reserve.[50] The Medical Officer in Umvuma reported the worst year on record for kwashiorkor (protein deficiency) among infants. 'Many arrived in hospital almost moribund', he wrote. 'You do not have to go to the Congo to see frank starvation of children.'[51] Deaths from malnutrition or kwashiorkor reported by Native Commissioners numbered 115 in Salisbury District (as against 76 in 1959), 29 in Mazoe, 23 in Que Que, 14 in Urungwe, 11 in Filabusi, 11 in Gwelo (as against 28 in 1959), 10 in Wedza, 7 in Chipinga, 3 in Goromonzi, 3 in Gutu, and 2 in Ndanga.[52] Yet malnutrition was widespread even in good years. In 1954 the nine leading government hospitals admitting Africans took in some 475 cases of kwashiorkor.[53] An investigator from the World Health Organization was struck in 1956 by the prevalence of malnutrition among rural schoolchildren. Professor Gelfand at Salisbury Hospital also concluded that malnutrition among Shona was worst in the Reserves and on European farms, although he thought the most common form was marasmus (calorie deficiency), found in adults (chiefly women) as well as children.[54] In 1958 the government's food technologist reported that the Land Husbandry Act had worsened nutrition in Chilimanzi District by reducing the herds and discouraging vegetable gardens.[55] 'There is little doubt', the Nutrition Council concluded at that time, 'that the incidence of malnutrition among Africans, particularly Kwashiorkor, is rising'. That was almost its last word on the subject, however, for after eleven years of inaction, due chiefly to the denial of funds by the European-controlled legislature, the Council dissolved itself in 1958, declaring, 'The nutrition of the African population has gone from bad to worse during the Council's frustrated existence'.[56] Malnutrition among the poor had replaced death by starvation as Southern Rhodesia's chief problem of subsistence. By the mid-1980s one of every six children under five years old was malnourished.[57]

The pattern of scarcity displayed in 1960 was to survive in Southern Rhodesia and Zimbabwe until at least the mid-1980s. Indeed, the more frequent incidence of scarcity after 1960 suggested not only that rainfall was worse than in the prosperous 1950s but that agrarian misery was deepening and the crisis of settler capitalism was worsening. By the late 1970s the Reserves carried three times as many people as they could support and the colony's per capita food production had fallen by nearly one-fifth since the early 1960s.[58] There was serious scarcity in 1964, 1965, 1970, 1980, 1982, 1983, 1984, and in some areas in 1986 and 1987.[59] During the drought of 1982-4 over 2 100 000 people received food relief.[60] A detailed study of suffering and relief in four villages of Chibi District at that time illustrated the further development of the patterns which this book has traced through the colonial period. Despite harvest failure, there was little overall shortage of food in Chibi during 1983-4, thanks to the excellent distribution system. Yet there were many hungry households, and they were the poor. Poverty in Chibi meant lack of access to cash income, chiefly from migrant labour. The poorest households, who suffered most during the drought, were those of widows or of separated, abandoned, or divorced mothers. 'Without cattle or cash income', the researcher found, 'eking out survival on such informal sector jobs as brewing beer and prostitution these households are closest to total destitution.'[61] For poor households — defined as those whose heads earned less than the national minimum wage — the government organized a relief programme administered by the Grain Marketing Board, the Ministry of Social Services, and ZANU(PF). This system worked quite well in Chibi. It was less satisfactory in Matabeleland, for there the drought was worsened by violence. Not only were colonial patterns still evident in the scarcity of 1982-4, but so were echoes from the nineteenth century.

# CHAPTER 12

## Conclusion

The peoples of pre-colonial Zimbabwe suffered recurrent scarcity but normally prevented it from causing numerous deaths. 'Famines that killed' appear to have occurred when violence intensified scarcity. This pattern survived into the early colonial period, but when the strains of colonial change began to reinforce the effects of drought, the government created a new system of famine relief which operated most fully in 1922. Thereafter, however, the growing dominance of settler capitalism changed the nature of famine and its relief. Famine in peripheral districts gave way to scarcity in areas of intensive White settlement, especially Matabeleland. The Maize Control Board, with its European suppliers and distributors, replaced the Native Affairs Department as relief agency. This system still operated in 1960, but by then settler capitalism found it increasingly difficult to prevent or relieve scarcity among a more numerous and impoverished African population.

The crisis of capitalism apparent in the scarcity of 1960 probably reappeared in all the numerous shortages of the next 25 years, but this book ends in 1960 because its chief sources — the records of the colonial government — are not yet available thereafter. It is important to stress in this conclusion how narrowly-based those sources are. Much research remains to be done on the history of famine in Zimbabwe, from both private papers, oral traditions, and, if possible, mortality statistics. Such research will probably destroy many of the arguments presented here. Moreover, there is no reason to think that Zimbabwe's famine history is any guide to those of other African countries. Each requires its own investigation.

This book may serve a purpose by providing a preliminary history of famine in one country. But it does not serve the purpose for which the research was undertaken. The original hypothesis was that famine and its control might be the key to Zimbabwe's remarkable population history, explaining why the population was so small in 1890, why it grew so soon thereafter, and why it grew so much during the colonial period as a whole. The evidence of this book is that the original hypothesis was false. In Zimbabwe — although not necessarily elsewhere in Africa — famine mortality was not the main constraint on pre-colonial population. Control of famine mortality in the colonial period cannot explain why population grew so early in the twentieth century. But colonial innovations can largely explain how population continued to grow so rapidly without suffering disastrous famine mortality. That is why the study of twentieth-century methods of preventing mortality is not 'highly specious', as Dr Watts has complained,[1] but highly relevant.

Nevertheless, the problem of Zimbabwe's population history remains largely unsolved. It is one of the most important, fascinating, and difficult problems presented by the country's history.

# Note on Rainfall Statistics

The source for early rainfall data in Zimbabwe is the official *Rainfall Handbook* (Salisbury, 1951) and its *Supplements 1-5*. These list annual totals (calculated from 1 July to 30 June) for many stations from the first records at Hope Fountain Mission (south of Bulawayo) in 1888/9 to 1945/6. In addition to Hope Fountain, I have used tables for Salisbury (from 1891/2), Bulawayo (1896/7), Fort Victoria (1899/1900), Mount Darwin (1901/2), and Victoria Falls (1904/5). For 1946/7 and 1947/8 I have used annual totals published in the *Bulawayo Chronicle* of 4 April 1947 and 9 April 1948. (These may omit a few drops falling after the dates of publication, but nothing significant.) From 1948/9 to 1961/2 I have taken figures from duplicated monthly *Climatological Surveys* (later *Meteorological Summaries)* published by the Rhodesia and Nyasaland Meteorological Service. The average annual rainfall for each station calculated from these figures was:

| | |
|---|---|
| Hope Fountain (1888/9-1945/6) | 674 mm (26,30 inches) |
| Salisbury (1891/2-1961/2) | 825 mm (32,18 inches) |
| Bulawayo (1896/7-1961/2) | 604 mm (23,57 inches) |
| Fort Victoria (1899/1900-1961/2) | 637 mm (24,85 inches) |
| Mount Darwin (1901/2-1961/2) | 786 mm (30,66 inches) |
| Victoria Falls (1904/5-1945/6) | 696 mm (27,15 inches) |

# Abbreviations

| | |
|---|---|
| Adm. | Administrator/Administration |
| Ann. | Annual |
| *Bulawayo Chron.* | *Bulawayo Chronicle* |
| B.S.A.Co. | British South Africa Company |
| C.N.C. | Chief Native Commissioner |
| Counc. World Miss. (M) | Council for World Mission (Matabeleland papers) [records at SOAS] |
| *Her.* | *Herald* |
| Methodist Miss. Soc. | Methodist Missionary Society [records at SOAS] |
| Mon. | Monthly |
| N.C. | Native Commissioner |
| P.N.C. | Provincial Native Commissioner |
| Q. | Quarterly |
| Rep. | Report (of/on etc.) |
| Rhod. | Rhodesia |
| Secr. N. Affs. | Secretary for Native Affairs |
| Sess. Pap. | Sessional Paper |
| Supt. N. | Superintendent of Natives |
| SOAS | School of Oriental and African Studies, London |
| South. | Southern |
| *Zambesi Miss. Rec.* | *Zambesi Mission Record* (London) |

Note: All archival references are to files in the National Archives of Zimbabwe, Harare, unless otherwise indicated (file numbers marked with an asterisk (*) are provisional)

# Notes

CHAPTER 1

1. South. Rhod., *Returns of a Census Taken on 17th April, 1904* (Sess. Pap. A.23, 1904), 6–7; Rhod., *Census of Population 1969* (Salisbury, Central Statistical Office, [1971?]), 6.
2. World Bank, *World Development Report 1986* (New York, The Bank, 1986), 180.
3. South. Rhod., *Rep. Director of Census, regarding the Census Taken on 7th May, 1911* (Sess. Pap. A.7, 1912), 25; D. N. Beach, 'Zimbabwean Demography: Early Colonial Data' (Milwaukee, Conference on the Analysis of Census Data from Colonial Central Africa, 1986), 8.
4. Rhod., *Census of Population 1969*, 5.
5. This was the conclusion of R. R. Kuczynski, *Demographic Survey of the British Colonial Empire* (London, Royal Inst. of Int. Affs, 3 vols., 1948-53), II, 123.
6. J. C. Miller, 'The significance of drought, disease and famine in the agriculturally marginal zones of West-Central Africa', *The Journal of African History* (1982), XXIII, 22.
7. D. N. Beach, 'The Shona economy: Branches of production', in R. H. Palmer and Q. N. Parsons (eds.), *The Roots of Rural Poverty in Central and Southern Africa* (London, Heinemann, 1977), 43–4.

8. R. C. Dutt, *Open Letters to Lord Curzon on Famines and Land Assessments in India* (London, Kegan Paul, 1900), 17. See also B. M. Bhatia, *Famines in India (1860–1965)* (London, Asia Publishing House, 2nd edn, 1967); H. S. Srivastava, *The History of Indian Famines and Development of Famine Policy (1858–1918)* (Agra, Mehra, 1968).

9. See A. Sen, *Poverty and Famines* (Oxford, Clarendon Press, revised edn, 1982); P. R. Greenough, *Prosperity and Misery in Modern Bengal: The Famine of 1943–1944* (New York, Oxford Univ. Press, 1982).

10. M. Watts, *Silent Violence: Food, Famine and Peasantry in Northern Nigeria* (Berkeley CA, Univ. of California Press, 1983), 272. For a similar analysis, see J. McCann, *From Poverty to Famine in Northeast Ethiopia: A Rural History 1900–1935* (Philadelphia, Univ. of Pennsylvania Press, 1987).

11. M. B. McAlpin, *Subject to Famine: Food Crisis and Economic Change in Western India, 1860–1920* (Princeton, Univ. Press, 1983).

12. See L. Brennan, 'The development of the Indian famine codes', in B. Currey and G. Hugo (eds.), *Famine as a Geographical Phenomenon* (Dordrecht, D. Reidel, 1984), 91–111.

13. K. Wrightson, *English Society 1580–1680* (London, Hutchinson, 1982), 146; F. Braudel and E. Labrousse (eds.), *Histoire économique et sociale de la France II* (Paris, Presses Univ. de France, 1970), 74–6; J. D. Post, 'Famine, mortality, and epidemic disease in the process of modernization', *Economic History Review* (1976), XXIX (2nd ser.), 14.

14. L. M. Li, 'Famine and famine relief: Viewing Africa in the 1980s from China in the 1920s', in M. H. Glantz (ed.), *Drought and Hunger in Africa* (Cambridge, Univ. Press, 1987), 415–34.

15. I. Klein, 'When the rains failed: Famine, relief, and mortality in British India', *Indian Economic and Social History Review* (1984), XXI, 189.

16. The point was made by M. Wilson in *South African Outlook* (1976), CVI, 41–2.

17. See A. Shepherd, 'Case Studies of famine: Sudan; in D. Curtis, M. Hubbard and A. Shepherd, *Preventing Famine: Policies and Prospects for Africa* (London, Routledge, 1988), ch. 3. See also D. F. Bryceson, 'Colonial famine responses: The Bagamoyo district of Tanganyika, 1920–61', *Food Policy* (1981), VI, ii, 91–104.

18. J. Iliffe, *The African Poor: A History* (Cambridge, Univ. Press, 1987), 159.

19. See M. Vaughan, *The Story of an African Famine: Gender and Famine in Twentieth-century Malawi* (Cambridge, Univ. Press, 1987).

20. David Beach suggested this to me early in my research but I then brushed it aside.

21. See Great Britain, *Report of the Indian Famine Commission: Part 3: Famine Histories* [C. 3086] (H. C. 1881, lxxi), part 1, 210.

CHAPTER 2

1. S. Lineham, 'Rainfall in Rhodesia', in M. O. Collins (ed.), *Rhodesia: Its Natural Resources and Economic Development* (Salisbury, M. O. Collins, 1965), 26–7.

2. Ibid.

3. J. Despois, *La Tunisie orientale: Sahel et basse steppe* (Paris, Publications de la Faculté des Lettres d'Alger, 1940), 59.

4. Quoted in D. N. Beach, *Zimbabwe before 1900* (Gweru, Mambo Press, 1984), 39.

5. T. M. Thomas, *Eleven Years in Central South Africa* (London, F. Cass, 2nd edn, 1971), 76.

6. D. Carnegie, *Among the Matabele* (London, Religious Tract Soc., 2nd edn, 1894), 24.

7. For natural regions, see G. Kay, *Rhodesia: A Human Geography* (London, Univ. of London Press, 1970), 13–19.

8. See the map in D. Birmingham and P. M. Martin (eds.), *History of Central Africa* (London, Longman, 2 vols., 1983), I, 249.

9. J. K. Rennie, 'Christianity, Colonialism and the Origins of Nationalism among the Ndau of Southern Rhodesia 1890–1935' (Evanston ILL, Northwestern Univ., Ph.D. thesis, 1973), 39–40, 53–4.

10. There is an excellent description of Shona agriculture in M. Gelfand, *Diet and Tradition in an African Culture* (Edinburgh, Livingstone, 1971), ch. 5.
11. W. Roder, 'The division of land resources in Southern Rhodesia', *Annals of the Association of American Geographers* (1964), LIV, 44.
12. *Zambesi Miss. Rec.* (1910-11), IV (Jan. 1911), 188–92.
13. H. N. Hemans, *The Log of a Native Commissioner* (London, H. F. & G. Witherby, 1935), 121–2. Thomas (*Eleven Years*, 379) gave a similar description in 1867.
14. D. N. Beach, 'Second thoughts on the Shona economy', *Rhodesian History* (1976), VII, 5; Carnegie, *Among the Matabele*, 25.
15. W. Roder, *The Sabi Valley Irrigation Projects* (Chicago, Univ. of Chicago, Dep. of Geography, 1965), 61; J. P. R. Wallis (ed.), *The Northern Goldfields Diaries of Thomas Baines* (London, Chatto & Windus, 3 vols., 1946), II, 295.
16. See T. Scudder, *Gathering among African Woodland Savannah Cultivators: A Case Study: The Gwembe Tonga* (Manchester, Manchester Univ. Press, 1971).
17. Beach, 'Second thoughts on the Shona economy', 5.
18. Carnegie, *Among the Matabele*, 25–6.
19. J. Kendal, 'Father Hartmann's notes', *NADA* (1945), XXII, 17.
20. A. C. Hodza and G. Fortune (eds.), *Shona Praise Poetry* (Oxford, Clarendon Press, 1979), 9.
21. See M. F. C. Bourdillon, *The Shona Peoples* (Gweru, Mambo Press, revised edn, 1982), ch. 10; A. K. H. Weinrich, *The Tonga People on the Southern Shore of Lake Kariba* (Gwelo, Mambo Press, 1977), 77–84.
22. E. Colson, *Social Organisation of the Gwembe Tonga* (Manchester, Manchester Univ. Press, 1960), 56; Roder, *The Sabi Valley Irrigation Projects,* 70; J. R. D. Cobbing, 'The Ndebele under the Khumalos, 1820–1896' (Lancaster, Univ. of Lancaster, Ph.D. thesis, 1976), 186.
23. Beach, 'The Shona economy', 56; Beach, *Zimbabwe before 1900*, 23.
24. Beach, 'Zimbabwean Demography', 7. For Mozambique, see G. J. Liesegang, 'Famines, epidemics, plagues and long periods of warfare: Their effects in Mozambique 1700–1975' (Harare, Univ. of Zimbabwe, Conference on Zimbabwean History, 1982). For smallpox, see M. H. Dawson, 'Socio-economic and Epidemiological Change in Kenya: 1880–1925' (Madison, Univ. of Wisconsin-Madison, Ph.D. thesis, 1983), ch. 1.
25. D. P. Abraham, 'The early political history of the Kingdom of Mwene Mutapa (850–1589)', in *Historians in Tropical Africa: Proceedings of the Leverhulme Inter-Collegiate History Conference* (Salisbury, Univ. College of Rhod. and Nyasaland, 1962), 64.
26. Ibid., 87, n. 67.
27. Francisco de Sousa, *Oriente Conquistado a Jesu Christo* (Lisbon, V. da Costa Deslandes, 2 parts, 1710), I, 866.
28. H. H. K. Bhila, *Trade and Politics in a Shona Kingdom* (Harlow, Longman, 1982), 48; A. da Silva Rego and E. E. Burke (eds.), *Documents on the Portuguese in Mozambique and Central Africa, 1497–1840* (Salisbury, National Archives of Rhod., 8 vols. to date, 1962- ),VIII, 237, 241, 247.
29. Beach, 'The Shona economy', 43.
30. Bhila, *Trade and Politics in a Shona Kingdom,* 164.
31. S. E. Nicholson, 'A Climatic Chronology for Africa' (Madison, Univ. of Wisconsin-Madison, Ph.D. thesis, 1976), 146.
32. See G. Liesegang, 'Nguni migrations between Delagoa Bay and the Zambezi, 1821–1839', *International Journal of African Historical Studies* (1970), III, 317–37.
33. D. P. Abraham, 'The principality of Maungwe', *NADA* (1951), XXVIII, 68.
34. J. Chidziwa, 'History of the Vashawasha', *NADA* (1964), IX, i, 26. Zwangendaba was an Nguni leader.
35. P. Forrestall, 'Chibi tribe', *NADA* (1970), X, ii, 85.
36. J. P. R. Wallis (ed.), *The Matabele Journals of Robert Moffat, 1829–1860* (London, Chatto &

Windus, 2 vols., 1945), II, 107.
37. S.O.A.S., Counc. World Miss., (M) 1/1/B/7, R. Moffat to Tidman, 26 Dec. 1859.
38. Ibid., (M) 2/1/A/3, Thomas to Directors, 10 Dec. 1860.
39. Ibid., (M) 1/1/D/20, Sykes to Tidman, 20 Sept. 1861.
40. E. C. Tabler, The Far Interior (Cape Town, A. A. Balkema, 1955), 120.
41. J. P. R. Wallis (ed.), The Matabele Mission (London, Chatto & Windus, 1945), 164.
42. S.O.A.S., Counc. World Miss., (M) 1/2/A/27, Sykes to Tidman, 29 July 1862; (M) 1/2/A/28, Thomas to Tidman, 23 Sept. 1862.
43  N/9/4/25, f. 708, Mon. Rep. Gutu, Nov. 1912.
44. See J. Iliffe, 'The poor in the modern history of Malawi', in K. J. McCracken (ed.), Malawi: An Alternative Pattern of Development (Edinburgh, Univ. of Edinburgh, Centre of African Studies, [1985]), 251–2; E. C. Mandala, 'Capitalism, Ecology and Society: The Lower Tchiri (Shire) Valley of Malawi, 1860–1960' (Minneapolis, Univ. of Minnesota, Ph.D. thesis, 1983), 63–6.
45. J. P. R. Wallis (ed.), The Southern African Diaries of Thomas Leask 1865–1870 (London, Chatto & Windus, 1954), 108; E. E. Burke (ed.), The Journals of Carl Mauch (Salisbury, National Archives of Rhod., 1969), 214; S.O.A.S., Counc. World Miss., (M) 1/3/D/77, Sykes to Whitehouse, 4 Jan. 1883; (M) 2/3/B, Helm to Thompson, 9 Feb. 1885; (M) 1/4/A/84, Carnegie to Thompson, 12 Aug. 1887; (M) 1/4/B/98, Helm to Thompson, 20 Dec. 1889.
46. S. E. Nicholson, 'The methodology of historical climate reconstruction and its application to Africa', The Journal of African History (1979), XX, 48.
47. Miller, 'The significance of drought, disease and famine', 19.
48. M. Gelfand (ed.), Gubulawayo and beyond: Letters and Journals of the Early Jesuit Missionaries to Zambesia (1879–1887) (London, G. Chapman, 1968); M. Lloyd (transl.), 'Diaries of the Jesuit missionaries at Bulawayo 1879–1881', Rhodesiana (1959), IV, 7–84.
49. Carnegie, Among the Matabele, 24; M. A. Hamutyinei and A. B. Plangger, Tsumo-Shumo: Shona Proverbial Lore and Wisdom (Gwelo, Mambo Press, 1974), 338.
50. W. Edwards, 'The Wanoe: A short historical sketch', NADA (1926), IV, 15.
51. Burke, The Journals of Carl Mauch, 173, 207, 214, 238; N/9/4/25, f. 708, Mon. Rep. Gutu, November 1912; Beach, 'The Shona economy', 39.
52. D. Chanaiwa, 'A History of the Nhowe before 1900' (Los Angeles, Univ. of California, Ph.D. thesis, 1971), 146.
53. Rep. Secr. N. Affs., C.N.C., 1942, in South. Rhod., Reps. Secr. N. Affs. and C.N.C., 1941, 1942, 1943, 1944 and 1945 (Sess. Pap. C.S.R.10, 1947), 53. See aslo S. H. Fynes-Clinton (ed.), 'Mavunga Madziwadzira: Headman Madzima recalls', NADA (1970), X, ii, 32, 34; R. C. Woollacott, 'Pasipamire — Spirit medium of Chaminuka', NADA (1975), XI, ii, 159; Chidziwa, 'History of the Vashawasha', 29; F. W. T. Posselt, Fact and Fiction (Bulawayo, Rhodesian Printing and Publishing, 1935), 204.
54. F. Johnson, Great Days (London, G. Bell, 1940), 60.
55. D. N. Beach, 'The initial impact of Christianity on the Shona', in A. J. Dachs (ed.), Christianity South of the Zambezi : I (Gwelo, Mambo Press, 1973), 31–2.
56. For the connection between drought, violence, and mortality, see also J. E. Inikori, 'Underpopulation in nineteenth-century West Africa: The role of the export slave trade', in C. Fyfe and D. McMaster (eds.), African Historical Demography : II (Edinburgh, Univ. of Edinburgh, Centre of African Studies, 1981), 297.

CHAPTER 3

1. 'Report on the Matabeleland Rebellion, by Earl Grey', Nov. 1896, in Great Britain, Report by Sir R. E. R. Martin . . . on the Native Administration of the British South Africa Company [C. 8547] (H. C. 1897, lxii), 629.
2. S.O.A.S., Counc. World Miss., (M) 2/4/A and 2/4/B, Rees to Thompson, 15 Dec. 1890 and 12

May 1891; Cobbing, 'The Ndebele under the Khumalos', 187.

3. S.O.A.S., Counc. World Miss., (M) 2/4/C, Helm to Thompson, 8 Jan. 1892; (M) 1/2/D/60, Thomson to Mullens, 14 Aug. 1871.

4. Cobbing, 'The Ndebele under the Khumalos', 383.

5. S.O.A.S., Counc. World Miss. (M) 2/5/C, Helm to Thompson, 9 Feb. 1895.

6. Quoted in S. P. Olivier, *Many Treks Made Rhodesia* (Cape Town, Timmins, 1957), 118. See also Beach, 'The Shona economy', 43; Taberer to N.C.s, 11 Sept. 1895, in Great Britain, *Rep. by Sir R. E. R. Martin*, 595; N/9/1/1, Ann. Rep. Chilimanzi 1895.

7. *Bulawayo Chron.*, 27 June 1896; L05/4/2, f. 394, Meredith to [C.N.C.?], 3 Mar. 1897; Edwards, 'The Wanoe', 20.

8. *Bulawayo Chron.*, 11 Jan., 4 Mar., 28 Mar., 1 Feb. 1896.

9. NB/6/1/1, Ann. Rep. Bubi 1897; LO/5/6/5, f. 202, Gordon to N.C. Bulawayo, 10 Oct. 1896; *Bulawayo Chron.*, 18 Apr. 1896.

10. LO/5/6/5, f. 126, Jackson to Supt. N. Bulawayo, 30 Sept. 1896. See also F. C. Selous, *Sunshine and Storm in Rhodesia* (London, Rowland Ward, 1896), 52, 118–19.

11. T. O. Ranger, *Revolt in Southern Rhodesia 1896–7* (London, Heinemann, 1967), 105–14; D. N. Beach, 'The Rising in South-western Mashonaland, 1896–7' (London, Univ. of London, Ph.D. thesis, 1971), ch. 5.

12. R. H. Palmer, *Land and Racial Domination in Rhodesia* (London, Heinemann, 1977), 28–42; S.O.A.S., Counc. World Miss., (M) 2/5/B, Carnegie to Thompson, 6 Apr. 1894; Selous, *Sunshine and Storm*, x.

13. R. H. Palmer, 'The agricultural history of Rhodesia', in Palmer and Parsons, *The Roots of Rural Poverty*, 227–30; Olivier, *Many Treks*, chs. 3, 4; D. N. Beach, 'Afrikaner and Shona settlement in the Enkeldoorn area, 1890-1900', *Zambezia* (1969-70), I, ii, 25–34.

14. Cobbing, 'The Ndebele under the Khumalos', 386.

15. R. S. S. Baden-Powell, *The Matabele Campaign* (London, Methuen, 4th edn, 1901), 186.

16. S.O.A.S., Counc. World Miss., (M) 1/5/C, Carnegie to Thompson, 5 June 1896.

17. Ibid., Reed to Thompson, 19 July 1896.

18. Ibid., Carnegie to Thompson, 24 July 1896.

19. J. Guy, *The Destruction of the Zulu Kingdom* (London, Longman, 1979), 243.

20. Baden-Powell, *The Matabele Campaign*, 232.

21. *Bulawayo Chron.*, 5 Sept. 1896.

22. H. Plumer, *An Irregular Corps in Matabeleland* (London, Kegan Paul, 1897), 195–6.

23. *Bulawayo Chron.*, 3 Oct. 1896.

24. Ibid., 14 Mar. and 10 Oct. 1896.

25. LO/5/6/5, f. 168, Grey to B.S.A.Co., 11 Oct. 1896.

26. LO/5/6/7, f. 74, Carrington to Deputy Commissioner, 23 Nov. 1896.

27. 'Report . . . by Earl Grey', Nov. 1896, in Great Britain, *Rep. by Sir R. E. R. Martin*, 632.

28. *Bulawayo Chron.*, 29 Aug. 1896.

29. LO/5/6/7, f. 235, H. J. Taylor, 'Report of the CNC's tour of inspection', [Dec. 1896] .

30. Ibid., f. 81, Mullins to C.N.C., 21 Nov. 1896

31. Ibid., f. 23, H. J. Taylor, 'Report on native affairs generally in Matabeleland', 9 Nov 1896.

32. LO/5/6/8, f. 350, Gielgud to C.N.C., 20 Mar. 1897.

33. C. L. Carbutt, 'Reminiscences of a Native Commissioner', *NADA* (1924), II, 79.

34. S.O.A.S., Counc. World Miss., (M) 2/6/A, Carnegie to Thompson, 20 Sept. 1896.

35. LO/5/6/8, f. 217, Gielgud to C.N.C., 5 Feb. 1897.

36. Lady Grey to her son, 23 Oct. 1896, quoted in R. Blake, *A History of Rhodesia* (London, Eyre Methuen, 1977), 137.

37. LO/5/6/5, f. 195, James Mkiza, statement, 10 Oct. 1896.

38. LO/5/6/9, ff. 52, 175, Mon. Rep. Malema, Apr. 1897, and Mon. Rep. Mzingwane, May 1897; *Bulawayo Chron.*, 12 Dec. 1896 and 9 Jan. 1897.

39. *Bulawayo Chron.*, 20 Feb. 1897.

40. LO/5/6/5, f. 247, Rhodes to Grey, 9 Oct. 1896,
41. B.S.A.Co., *Rep. Company's Proceedings and the Condition of the Territories within the Sphere of Its Operations, 1896–1897 ([London, The Company, 1898])*, 91, 94.
42. LO/5/6/8, f. 33, 'Meeting of the headmen and indunas at Bulawayo, 5th January, 1897'.
43. *Bulawayo Chron.*, 24 Dec. 1896 and 13 Feb. 1897; S.O.A.S., Methodist Miss. Soc., 333/3/54, Eva to Hartley, 12 Dec. 1896.
44. *Bulawayo Chron.*, 13 Feb. 1897.
45. S.O.A.S., Methodist Miss. Soc., 333/3/54, Eva to Hartley, 12 Dec. 1896; *Bulawayo Chron.*, 9 and 30 Jan., and 6 Feb. 1897.
46. LO/5/6/9, f. 156, Griffith to C.N.C., 2 June 1897.
47. LO/5/6/6, f. 353, Gielgud to C.N.C., 30 Oct. 1896; LO/5/6/7, f. 132, id. to id., 29 Nov. 1896; LO/5/6/8, f. 120, id. to id., 20 Jan. 1897.
48. LO/5/6/9, f. 47, Gielgud to C.N.C., 3 Apr. 1897.
49. NB/6/1/1, Gielgud to C.N.C., 26 Mar. 1898.
50. LO/5/6/8, f. 276, Mon. Rep. Umzingwane, February 1897; S.O.A.S., Counc. World Miss., (M) 2/6/B, Reed to Thompson, 1 Jan. 1897; *Zambesi Miss. Rec.* (1922-5), VII (Apr. 1923), 207.
51. LO/5/6/7, f. 247, Moodie to C.N.C., 14 Dec. 1896.
52. LO/5/4/3, f. 340, Campbell to C.N.C., 15 May 1897.
53. These actions are listed in E. A. H. Alderson, *With the Mounted Infantry and the Mashonaland Field Force 1896* (London, Methuen, 1898), 278–95.
54. LO/5/4/1, f. 218, Taberer to Adm., 18 Dec. 1896.
55. Quoted in J. J. Taylor, 'The Emergence and Development of the Native Department in Southern Rhodesia, 1894–1914' (London, Univ. of London, Ph.D. thesis, 1974), 94.
56. LO/5/4/1, f. 312, F. Richartz, 'Some particulars about the attitude of the Natives in Chishwasha District', 10 Jan. 1897; ibid., f. 449, Meredith to C.N.C., 6 Jan 1897.
57. H. Marshall Hole, 'The Mashonaland rebellion', in B.S.A.Co., *Reports on the Native Disturbances in Rhodesia 1896-7* (London, The Company, 1898), 119.
58. LO/5/4/4, f. 229, Campbell to C.N.C., 22 June 1897.
59. Fynes-Clinton, 'Mavunga Madziwadzira', 34.
60. B.S.A.Co., *Rep. 1896–1897*, 88.
61. J. W. Stanlake, 'Travelling in Mashonaland since the war', *Work and Workers in the Mission Field* (1898), VII, 14.

CHAPTER 4

1. Native Commissioners' monthly reports for 1903 survive from Mashonaland only; they are in N/9/4/14–17. A few annual reports from Mashonaland are in N/9/1/8 and NB/6/1/5; extracts were published in South. Rhod., *Rep. C.N.C., Mashonaland, for the Year Ended 31st March, 1904* (Sess. Pap. A.17, 1904). I have omitted most references to these documents, as in subsequent chapters.
2. Palmer, *Land and Racial Domination*, 24.
3. T. Scudder, *The Ecology of the Gwembe Tonga* (Manchester, Manchester Univ. Press, 1962), 215.
4. See M. H. Dawson, 'Disease and population decline of the Kikuyu of Kenya, 1890–1925', in Fyfe and McMaster, *African Historical Demography*, II, 128–9; L. Vail and L. White, *Capitalism and Colonialism in Mozambique* (London, Heinemann, 1980), 119–20.
5. Palmer, *Land and Racial Domination*, 59, 91; Taylor, 'The Emergence and Development of the Native Department', 268.
6. e.g. N/9/1/8, f. 147, Ann. Rep. Victoria 1902–3.
7. *Rhod. Her.*, 19 Sept. 1903.
8. S. P. Hyatt, *The Old Transport Road* (London, Andrew Melrose, 1914), 75–6. See also I. R. Phimister, 'Peasant production and underdevelopment in Southern Rhodesia, 1890–1914', in

119

9. N/9/1/5, Ann. Rep. Charter 1898–9; T. O. Ranger, *Peasant Consciousness and Guerrilla War in Zimbabwe* (London, James Currey, 1985), 31–3, 37–8; South. Rhod., *Rep. C.N.C., Matabeleland, for the Year Ended 31st March, 1901* (Sess. Paps., 1901), 4.
10. B.S.A.Co., *Rep. Adm. of Rhod., 1898–1900* ((London, [The Company, 1901]), 152, 161; South. Rhod., *Returns of a Census 1904*, 6–7; N/9/4/15, f. 120, Mon. Rep. Charter, June 1903.
11. Except in Makoni and Inyanga Districts.
12. *Rhod. Her.*, 3 Jan. 1903; *Zambesi Miss. Rec.* (1902-5), II (July 1903), 256.
13. N/9/1/8, ff. 45,54, Ann. Reps. Gutu and Hartley 1902–3.
14. *Rhod. Her.*, 25 July 1903.
15. N/9/4/16, f. 119, Mon. Rep. Inyanga, September 1903.
16. N/9/4/17, f. 123, Mon. Rep. Hartley, December 1903.
17. South. Rhod., *Rep. C.N.C., Mashonaland, for the Year Ended 31st March, 1904*, 2, 14.
18. A. S. Cripps, 'Les revenants', in his *Lyra Evangelistica: Missionary Verses of Mashonaland* (Oxford, B. H. Blackwell, 1909), 115. His experience of the famine is described in his letters in the papers of the United Society for the Propagation of the Gospel in Rhodes House, Oxford.
19. See above, 23; Roder, *The Sabi Valley Irrigation Projects*, 81.
20. N/9/1/8, f. 109, Ann. Rep. Melsetter 1902–3; South. Rhod., *Rep. C.N.C., Mashonaland, for the Year Ended 31st March, 1904*, 21.
21. N/9/4/15, f. 41, Mon. Rep. Melsetter, April 1903.
22. Ibid., f. 148, Mon. Rep. Melsetter, June 1903.
23. N/9/4/17, f. 66, Mon. Rep. Chibi, November 1903.
24. N/9/4/18, f. 29, Mon. Rep. Ndanga, January 1904.
25. N/9/4/16, f. 70, Mon. Rep. Lomagundi, August 1903.
26. W. E. Scott, 'Report of patrol to Zambesi' [late Sept. 1903] in Public Record Office, C[olonial] O[ffice] 879 [Confidential Print], 79 ['Further Correspondence Relative to Affairs in the Bechuanaland Protectorate and Rhodesia'] (cited hereafter as Africa (South), 717 ), 672.
27. N/9/4/17, f. 62, Mon. Rep. Lomagundi, November 1903.
28. NB/6/1/5, f. 67, Ann. Rep. Wankie 1903–4.
29. Ibid., f. 59, Ann. Rep. Sebungwe-Mafungabusi 1903–4.
30. N/9/4/18, f. 48, Mon. Rep. Lomagundi, January 1904.
31. Taylor, 'The Emergence and Development of the Native Department', 342.
32. Ibid., 174, n. 6.
33. N/9/4/15, f. 143, Mon. Rep. North Mazoe, June 1903.
34. N/9/4/16, f. 104. Mon. Rep. North Mazoe, August 1903.
35. *Rhod. Her.*, 5 Sept. 1903; D. N. Beach. 'Mapondera: The Career of a Hero of the Northern Zimbabwean Plateau, c. 1840–1904' (Harare, Univ. of Zimbabwe, History Dep., [1987]), 38.
36. N/9/4/17, f. 26, Mon. Rep. North Mazoe, October 1903.
37. NSC/1/1/1, Evidence in Mount Darwin Magistrate's Court, case 12, 3 Aug. 1914.
38. N/9/4/18, f. 60, Mon. Rep. North Mazoe, February 1904.
39. Ibid.
40. Ibid., f. 116, Mon. Rep. North Mazoe, March 1904.
41. N/9/1/8, f. 130, Ann. Rep. Ndanga 1902–3.
42. Ibid., f. 109, Ann. Rep. Melsetter 1902–3.
43. P. J. Duignan, 'Native Policy in Southern Rhodesia, 1890–1923' (Stanford CA, Stanford Univ., Ph.D. thesis, 1961), 261. For the procedures, see the entries for 1903 in NVA/3/1/1.
44. N/9/4/16, f. 114, Mon. Rep. Gutu, September 1903.
45. Ibid., f. 133, Mon. Rep. Melsetter, September 1903.
46. South. Rhod., *Rep. Public Health, for the Year Ended 31st March, 1904* (Sess. Pap. A.15, 1904), 5.
47. South. Rhod., *Rep. C.N.C., Mashonaland, for the Year Ended 31st March, 1904*, 25.
48. Ibid. , 2.
49. Scott, 'Report' [late September 1903] in Africa (South) 717, 672.

50. *Bulawayo Chron.*, 14 March 1903.
51. Quoted in Holland to B.S.A.Co., 14 May 1903, in Africa (South) 717, 555.
52. Ibid.
53. Milton, minute, 31 Aug. 1903, in ibid., 556.
54. N/9/4/17, f. 123, Mon. Rep. Hartley, December 1903.
55. N/9/4/16, f. 18, Mon. Rep. Lomagundi, July 1903; *Bulawayo Chron.*, 30 May 1903.
56. N/9/4/17, f. 90, Mon. Rep. Salisbury, November 1903.
57. N/9/4/15, f. 41, Mon. Rep. Melsetter, April 1903.
58. *Bulawayo Chron.*, 27 June 1903; P. Zachrisson, *An African Area in Change: Belingwe 1894–1946* (Gothenburg, Univ. of Gothenburg, 1978), 195.
59. Ranger, *Peasant Consciousness*, 40–2.
60. South. Rhod., *Rep. C.N.C., Mashonaland, for the Year Ended 31st March, 1904*, 2.
61. N/9/4/16, f. 70, Mon. Rep. Lomagundi, August 1903; N/9/4/17, f. 73, Mon. Rep. Hartley, November 1903.
62. Clarke to High Commissioner, 10 Sept. 1903, in Africa (South) 717, 555.
63. N/9/4/18, f. 14, Mon. Rep. Melsetter, January 1904.
64. N/9/4/15, f. 24, Mon. Rep. Lomagundi, April 1903.
65. N/9/1/8, f. 109, Ann. Rep. Melsetter 1902–3.
66. N/9/4/17, f. 26, Mon. Rep. North Mazoe, October 1903.
67. Ibid., f. 68, Mon. Rep. North Mazoe, November 1903.
68. Cripps, *Lyra Evangelistica*, 103.

CHAPTER 5

1. Native Commissioners' monthly reports for 1912 are in N/9/4/25; annual reports are in N/9/1/15 and NB/6/1/12.
2. See Iliffe, *The African Poor*, 157.
3. N/9/1/15, f. 129, Ann. Rep. Chibi 1912.
4. Ibid., ff. 32, 102, Ann. Reps. Darwin and Mtoko 1912.
5. B. A. Kosmin, '"Freedom, Justice and Commerce": Some factors affecting Asian trading patterns in Southern Rhodesia, 1897–1942', *Rhodesian History* (1975), VI, 23.
6. South. Rhod., *Rep. C.N.C., Mashonaland, for the Year Ended 31st December, 1909* (Sess. Pap. A.3, 1910), 2–3.
7. P. Mosley, *The Settler Economies: Studies in the Economic History of Kenya and Southern Rhodesia 1900–1963* (Cambridge, Univ. Press, 1983), 158–61.
8. South. Rhod., *Rep. C.N.C., Mashonaland, for the Year Ended 31st March, 1907* (Sess. Pap. A.3, 1907), 2.
9. Phimister, 'Peasant production and underdevelopment in Southern Rhodesia, 1890–1914', in Palmer and Parsons, *The Roots of Rural Poverty*, 262–3.
10. Ibid., 263.
11. Ibid.
12. *Bulawayo Chron.*, 21 Nov. 1912.
13. Phimister, 'Peasant production and underdevelopment in Southern Rhodesia, 1890–1914', f.118; *The Roots of Rural Poverty*, 264; N/9/1/15, Ann. Rep. Victoria 1912.
14. N/9/4/25, f. 50, Mon. Rep. Ndanga, January 1912.
15. Ibid., f. 204, Mon. Rep. Melsetter, March 1912.
16. N/9/1/15, f. 102, Ann. Rep. Mtoko 1912.
17. N/9/4/25, f. 144, Mon. Rep. Charter, March 1912.
18. N/9/1/15, f. 162, Ann. Rep. Ndanga 1912.
19. Palmer, *Land and Racial Domination*, 91.
20. Ibid., 92.
21. N/9/4/25, f. 255, Mon. Rep. Ndanga, April 1912.

22. South. Rhod., *Debates in the Legislative Counc., 1912*, cc. 203, 208, 20 May.
23. *Rhod. Her.*, 24 Mar. 1916.
24. Weekly figures in *Rhod. Her.*
25. Weekly figures in *Bulawayo Chron.*
26. N/9/1/15, f. 102, Ann. Rep. Mtoko 1912 ; N/9/4/25, ff. 60, 699, Mon. Reps. Makoni, January 1912, Victoria, November 1912; N/9/4/26, f. 40, Mon. Rep. Gutu, January 1913.
27. N/9/1/15, f. 162, Ann. Rep. Ndanga 1912.
28. N/9/4/26, f. 40, Mon. Rep. Gutu, January 1913.
29. N/9/1/15, f. 118, Ann. Rep. Victoria 1912.
30. N/9/4/25, f. 245, Mon. Rep. Chibi, April 1912.
31. N/3/11/1, f. 44, Hole to C.N.C., 21 May 1912.
32. N/9/4/25, f. 324, Mon. Rep. Ndanga, May 1912.
33. E. K. Mashingaidze, 'Christian Missions in Mashonaland, Southern Rhodesia, 1890–1930' (York, Univ. of York, Ph.D. thesis, 1973), 345, n. 2.
34. N/3/11/2, f. 44, N.C. Sinoia to Supt. N. Salisbury, 24 Aug. 1914.
35. N/9/4/25, f. 324, Mon. Rep. Ndanga, May 1912; NVB/1/1/1, f. 242, Blackwell to N.C. Ndanga, 4 May 1912.
36. N/3/11/1, f. 34, C. L. Carbutt, 'Report on scarcity of food supplies amongst natives in the Victoria Circle', 14 June 1912.
37. N/9/4/25, f. 379, Mon. Rep. Chibi, June 1912.
38. NVB/1/1/1, f. 343, Blackwell to N.C. Ndanga, 20 July 1912.
39. N/9/4/25, f. 512, Mon. Rep. Ndanga, August 1912.
40. N/3/11/1, f. 13, Bazeley to Supt. N. Victoria, 28 Aug. 1912.
41. A/3/18/22, f. 265, Bazeley to Supt. N. Victoria, 28 Aug. 1912.
42. N/9/1/15, f. 162, Ann. Rep. Ndanga 1912.
43. N/3/11/1, f. 13, Bazeley to Supt. N. Victoria, 28 Aug. 1912.
44. See J. B. Peires, 'Sir George Grey versus the Kaffir Relief Committee', *Journal of Southern African Studies* (1983–4), X, 145–69; W. Beinart, *The Political Economy of Pondoland, 1860–1930* (Cambridge, Univ. Press, 1982), 70–6. I am grateful to Dr Beinart for further information on this point.
45. Charles Trevelyan quoted in C. Woodham-Smith, *The Great Hunger: Ireland 1845–9* (reprinted, London, New English Library, 1968), 371.
46. A/3/18/22, f. 214, Milton to Hole, 9 Aug. 1912.
47. Ibid., f. 205, Taylor to Hole, 12 Aug. 1912, and Milton on this.
48. Ibid., f. 200, Holland to C.N.C. Bulawayo, 20 Aug. 1912.
49. A/3/18/23, f. 347, Masterman to Adm., 11 Sept. 1912.
50. N/9/4/25, f. 581, Mon. Rep. Ndanga, September 1912.
51. NVB/1/1/1, f. 399, Blackwell to N.C. Ndanga, 25 Oct. 1912.
52. A/3/18/22, f. 186, Masterman to Adm., 18 Oct. 1912.
53. Ibid., f. 239, Milton, minute, 19 Oct. 1912.
54. N/9/4/25, f. 649, Mon. Rep. Ndanga, Oct. 1912.
55. A/3/18/22, f. 131, Masterman to Adm., 27 Oct. 1912.
56. N/9/4/25, f. 649, Mon. Rep. Ndanga, October 1912.
57. A/3/18/22, f. 160, N.C.Melsetter to Ordnance Officer, 21 Oct. 1912,
58. Ibid., f. 137, Lenthall to N.C. Melsetter, n. d.
59. Ibid., f. 152, Masterman to Adm., 23 Oct. 1912.
60. Ibid., f. 124, Masterman to Adm., 7 Nov. 1912.
61. Ibid., f. 42, 'Extract from the monthly report of O. C. "D" Troop, Umtali', n. d.
62. N/9/4/25, f. 717, Mon. Rep. Ndanga, November 1912.
63. A/3/18/22, f. 76, Masterman to Adm., 28 Nov. 1912.
64. *Rhod. Her.*, 14 Nov. 1912.
65. A/3/18/22, f. 86, Milton to B.S.A.Co., n. d. [28 Nov. 1912].

66. Ibid., f. 1, Longden to Adm., 13 Jan. 1913.
67. N/9/4/25, f. 763, Mon. Rep. Chibi, December 1912.
68. Ibid., f. 773, Mon. Rep. Ndanga, December 1912.
69. NVB/1/1/1, f. 570, Blackwell to N.C. Ndanga, 2 May 1913.
70. Ibid., f. 539, Blackwell to N.C. Ndanga, 1 Apr. 1913.
71. N/9/4/26, f. 183, Mon. Rep. Melsetter, March 1913.
72. NB/6/1/12, ff. 48, 69, Ann. Reps. Insiza and Sebungwe 1912; South. Rhod., *Rep. Public Health, 1912* (Sess. Pap. A.1, 1914), 4–6, 14, 17–19, 28–9.
73. N/9/4/26, f. 160, Mon. Rep. Chibi, March 1913.
74. N/9/4/25, f. 291, Mon. Rep. Lomagundi, May 1912.
75. See C. Van Onselen, 'The 1912 Wankie Colliery strike', *The Journal of African History* (1974), XV, 275–89.
76. Scudder, *The Ecology of the Gwembe Tonga,* 215–16, 222.
77. South. Rhod., *Rep. C.N.C., Matabeleland, for the Year Ended 31st March, 1904* (Sess. Pap. A.14, 1904), 3. The Colonial Office filed correspondence about the famine of 1903 under the heading 'Food Shortage in Mashonaland'.
78. NB/6/1/12, f. 14, Ann. Rep. Bulalima Mangwe 1912.
79. Ibid., f. 1, Ann. Rep. Belingwe 1912.
80. *Zambesi Miss. Rec.* (1910-13), IV (July 1912), 406, and (Jan. 1913), 477.
81. South. Rhod., *Rep. C.N.C., Matabeleland, 1911* (Sess. Pap. A.3, 1912), 7.
82. NB/6/1/12, f. 29, Ann. Rep. Gwanda-Tuli 1912.
83. Ibid., f. 6, Ann. Rep. Bubi 1912.
84. South. Rhod., *Rep. C.N.C., Matabeleland, 1912* (Sess. Pap. A.3, 1913), 4.
85. Id. *1908* (Sess. Pap. A.4, 1909), 4; id. *1912,* 2.
86. Id. *1912,* 2.
87. *Zambesi Miss. Rec.* (1910-13), IV (July 1913), 549.
88. Ibid. (Apr. 1913), 514.
89. Ibid. (1914-17), V (July 1914), 83.
90. Ibid. (Jan. 1915), 156.
91. Ibid. (July 1915), 228.
92. A. J. Dachs, and W. F. Rea, *The Catholic Church and Zimbabwe 1879–1979* (Gwelo, Mambo Press, 1979), 63.
93. N/9/1/15, f. 129, Ann. Rep. Chibi 1912; South. Rhod., *Rep. C.N.C., Matabeleland, 1912,* 4; A/3/18/22, f. 20, Adm. to Resident Commissioner, 24 Dec. 1912.
94. A/3/18/22, f. 33, B.S.A.Co. to Adm., 21 Dec. 1912.
95. Ibid., f. 20, Adm. to Resident Commissioner, 24 Dec. 1912; A/3/18/23, f. 344, Masterman to Adm., 22 Jan. 1913. In 1922 the Treasurer said that the famine of 1912–13 had cost Government something over £50 000, of which all but £4 300 had been recovered. See South. Rhod., *Debates in the Legislative Counc., 1922,* c. 91, 8 May.

CHAPTER 6

1. Native Commissioners' monthly and annual reports for 1916 are in N/9/4/30–31 and N/9/1/19, respectively.
2. N/9/4/30, f. 71, Mon. Rep. C.N.C., February 1916; N/3/11/4, f. 145, Supt. N. Bulawayo to C.N.C., 1 Mar. 1916.
3. Mosley, *Settler Economies,* 120.
4. N/9/4/31, f. 222, Mon. Rep. Makoni, September 1916. See also Ranger, *Peasant Consciousness,* 28–49.
5. *Rhod. Her.,* 24 Nov. 1916; N/9/4/30, f. 125, Mon. Rep. Makoni, February 1916; N/9/1/19, f. 38, Ann. Rep. Lomagundi 1916.
6. N/9/1/19, f. 96, Thomas to C.N.C., 22 Jan. 1917.

7. Ibid., f. 205, Ann. Rep. Gwanda 1916.
8. N/9/4/30, f. 82, Mon. Rep. Darwin, February 1916.
9. N/9/1/19, f. 57, Ann. Rep. Mazoe 1916.
10. N/9/4/31, f. 77, Mon. Rep. Sebungwe-Mafungabusi, July 1916.
11. N/9/4/30, f. 546, Mon. Rep. Sebungwe-Mafungabusi, June 1916.
12. N/9/1/19, f. 263, Ann. Rep. Sebungwe 1916.
13. N/3/11/4, f. 24, F. Posselt to Supt. N. Bulawayo, 10 Nov. 1916.
14. Ibid.
15. N/9/4/31, f. 353, Mon. Rep. C.N.C., November 1916.
16. Zambesi Miss. Rec. (1914-17), V (Apr. 1917), 465.
17. N/3/11/4, f. 1, Taylor to Adm., 11 Dec. 1916.
18. Zachrisson, An African Area in Change: Belingwe, 155; Mosley, Settler Economies, 158.
19. N/9/4/30, f. 401, Mon. Rep. Gutu, May 1916.
20. NSA/2/4/1, J. W. Posselt to Supt. N. Salisbury, 17 Apr. 1916.
21. H. W. D. Longden, Red Buffalo (Cape Town, Juta, 1950), 64.
22. N/9/1/19, ff. 128, 6, 253, 189 and 205, Ann. Reps. Gutu, Buhera, Insiza, Bulalima-Mangwe and Gwanda, 1916.
23. N/9/1/19, f. 113, Ann. Rep. Chilimanzi 1916.
24. Rhod. Her., 1916, passim; above, 45.
25. N/9/4/30, f. 384, Mon. Rep. Mrewa, May 1916; N/9/4/31, f. 162, Mon. Rep. Selukwe, August 1916.
26. N/9/4/30, f. 454, Mon. Rep. Belingwe, May 1916; N/9/4/31, ff. 120, 225, Mon. Reps. Gutu, August 1916, Melsetter, September 1916.
27. I. R. Phimister, 'Meat and monopolies: Beef cattle in Southern Rhodesia, 1890–1938', The Journal of African History (1978), XIX, 401.
28. Rhod. Her., 1912 and 1916, passim.
29. N/9/1/19, ff. 30, 15, Ann. Reps. Hartley 1916, Charter 1916; N/3/11/4, f. 105, N.C. Gwanda to Supt. N. Bulawayo, 17 July 1916.
30. South. Rhod., Rep. C.N.C., 1916 (Sess. Pap. A.3, 1917), 9; Taylor, 'The Emergence and Development of the Native Department', 270.
31. Rhod. Her., 29 Dec. 1916; Palmer, Land and Racial Domination, 92; South. Rhod., Debates in the Legislative Counc., 1916, c. 19, 1 May .
32. Palmer, Land and Racial Domination, 92.
33. See above, 80.
34. Palmer, Land and Racial Domination, 88.
35. N/9/1/15, f. 189 and N/9/1/19, f. 160, Ann. Reps. Makoni 1912 and 1916
36. NB/6/1/12, f. 53 and N/9/1/19, f. 211, Ann. Reps. Matobo 1912 and 1916.
37. N/9/1/19, ff. 201, 222, Ann. Reps. Bulawayo and Mzingwani 1916.
38. N/3/11/5, f. 8, Oliver to N.C. Charter, 25 Nov. 1918.
39. N/9/1/19, f. 211, Ann. Rep. Matobo 1916.
40. South. Rhod., Debates in the Legislative Counc., 1922, c. 199, 11 May.
41. For Taylor, see R. Howman, 'Sir Herbert John Taylor, Kt.', Rhodesiana (Mar. 1977), XXXVI, 1–15.
42. See Watts, Silent Violence, 290–1, 308–14.
43. e.g. N/3/11/4, f. 55, Oliver to N.C. Charter, 20 Apr. 1916.
44. Ibid., f. 131, Adm. to C.N.C., 14 Mar. 1916.
45. NSA/2/4/1, Taylor to Supt. N. Salisbury, 8 Apr. 1916.
46. N/9/4/30, f. 263, Mon. Rep. Belingwe, March 1916.
47. M. Alamgir, Famine in South Asia (Cambridge MA, Oelgeschlager, Gunn & Hain, 1980), 70.
48. N/9/4/31, f. 343, Mon. Rep. Belingwe, October 1916.
49. N/3/11/4, f. 98, Jackson to C.N.C., 24 Aug. 1916.
50. M. B. McAlpin, Famine Relief Policy in India: Six Lessons for Africa (Providence, Centre for

the Comparative Study of Development, Working Paper 2, 1985), 2, 11–12.

51. *Rhod. Her.,* 17 Mar. 1916.
52. South. Rhod., *Rep. C.N.C., 1916,* 9; N/3/11/4, f. 1, Taylor to Adm., 11 Dec. 1916.
53. South. Rhod., *Rep. Public Health, 1919* (Sess. Pap. A.16, 1920), 23, 31.
54. N/3/11/4, f. 1, Taylor to Adm., 11 Dec. 1916.
55. N/3/11/3, f. 10, Bazeley to Supt. N. Victoria, 21 Aug. 1915.
56. N/9/4/30, f. 117, Mon. Rep. Ndanga, Feb. 1916.
57. NVB/1/1/2, f. 439, Watters to N.C. Ndanga, 26 Apr. 1916.
58. N/3/11/4, f. 8, Bazeley to Supt. N. Victoria, 25 Nov.1916.
59. N/9/4/30, f. 403, Mon. Rep. Ndanga, May 1916.
60. See 'Murombo', 'Old Bikita', *NADA* (1963), XL, 113–14.
61. NVB/1/2, f. 476, Watters to N.C. Ndanga, 5 June 1916.
62. Figures from N9/4/30–31, Mon. Reps.
63. N/9/4/31, f. 216, Mon. Rep. Bikita, September 1916,
64. N/3/11/4, f. 16, Watters to N.C. Ndanga, 16 Nov. 1916.
65. Ibid.; N9/1/19, f. 140, Ann. Rep. Ndanga 1916.
66. N/9/1/25, f. 155a, Ann. Rep. Ndanga 1922; N/9/4/43, f. 54, Mon. Rep. Ndanga, July 1922.
67. N/9/4/43, f. 1, Mon. Rep. C.N.C., July 1922.
68. NVB/1/1/2, f. 634, Watters to N.C. Ndanga, 16 Nov. 1916; N/9/1/19, f. 140, Ann. Rep. Ndanga 1916.
69. NVB/1/1/2, f. 634, Watters to N.C. Ndanga, 16 Nov. 1916.
70. 'African names of Native and District Commissioners', *NADA* (1976), XI, iii, 356.
71. NVB1/1/2, f. 498, Watters to N.C. Ndanga, 22 July 1916.

CHAPTER 7

1. Native Commissioners' monthly and annual reports for 1922 are in N/9/4/42–43 and N/9/1/25, respectively.
2. Mosley, *Settler Economies,* 120.
3. Ibid.
4. N/9/4/42, f. 168, C.N.C. Mon. Rep., March 1922; N/3/11/7/ff. 177, 209, Taylor to Adm., 11 Apr. 1922, and Bazeley to Supt. N. Umtali, 17 Mar. 1922.
5. For Gutu, see J. T. Bent, *The Ruined Cities of Mashonaland* (London, Longman, new edn, 1895), 258; N/9/1/25, f. 148, Ann. Rep. Gutu 1922.
6. N/9/4/42, ff. 218, 380, Mon. Reps. Gutu, March 1922, Marandellas, May 1922; South. Rhod., *Rep. Public Health,* 1922, 3, 11–12, 34–5.
7. J. M. Penvenne, 'A History of African Labour in Lourenço Marques, Mozambique, 1877 to 1950' (Boston, Boston Univ., Ph.D. thesis, 1982), 296.
8. N/9/1/24, f. 188, Ann. Rep. Supt. N. Bulawayo 1921.
9. *Rhod. Her.,* 1922, *passim;* above, 45, 60.
10. Palmer, *Land and Racial Domination,* 92.
11. N/9/1/25, f. 306, Ann. Rep. Gwelo 1922.
12. *Rhod. Her.,* 1912, 1916, 1922, *passim.*
13. *Rhod. Her.,* 28 July 1922.
14. N/9/4/42, f. 56, Mon. Rep. Gwanda, January 1922; N/3/11/7, f. 190, Thomas to Supt. N. Bulawayo, 24 Mar. 1922.
15. N/9/1/25, f. 313, Ann. Rep. Belingwe 1922.
16. N/3/11/6, ff. 30, 29, Edwards to Supt. N. Salisbury, 19 Jan. 1920, and Drew to Supt. N. Salisbury, 31 Jan. 1920.
17. N/9/1/25, f. 245, Ann. Rep. Supt. N. Bulawayo 1922.
18. N/3/11/8, f. 42, Jackson to C.N.C., 8 Jan. 1923.
19. N/9/4/42, f. 322, Mon. Rep. Gutu, April 1922.

20. N/9/1/25, f. 258, Ann. Rep. Bulalima-Mangwe 1922.
21. N/9/4/43, f. 520, Mon. Rep. Lomagundi, November 1922.
22. Ibid., f. 376, Mon. Rep. Sipolilo, October 1922.
23. N/3/11/8, f. 42, Jackson to C.N.C., 8 Jan. 1923.
24. N/9/1/25, f. 90, Ann. Rep. Mtoko 1922; N/9/4/43, f. 289, Mon. Rep. Bikita, September 1922; N/9/1/25, f. 254, Ann. Rep. Bubi 1922; N/3/11/7, f. 100, Jackson to C.N.C., 21 Aug. 1922.
25. N/9/1/25, f. 43, Ann. Rep. Sipolilo 1922.
26. Ibid., f. 258, Ann. Rep. Bulalima-Mangwe 1922.
27. S.O.A.S., Methodist Miss. Soc., 827/11, Butler to Burnet, 28 July 1922.
28. Mosley, *Settler Economies,* 158–9.
29. N/9/1/25, ff. 205, 64, Ann. Reps. Inyanga and Mazoe 1922.
30. *Zambesi Miss. Rec.* (1922-5), VII (Apr. 1922), 41.
31. Roder, *The Sabi Valley Irrigation Projects,* 93–9.
32. N/9/4/42, f. 324, Mon. Rep. Ndanga, April 1922.
33. South. Rhod., *Rep. C.N.C. 1922* (Sess. Pap. A.5, 1923), 6.
34. Roder, 'The division of land resources', 51.
35. N/9/1/19, f. 156, N/9/1/25, f. 205, Ann. Reps. Inyanga 1916 and 1922; N/9/1/19, f. 175, N/9/1/25, f. 190, Ann. Reps. Umtali 1916 and 1922; N/9/1/19, f. 15, N/9/1/25, f. 10, Ann. Reps. Charter 1916 and 1922.
36. N/9/1/19, f. 211, N/9/1/25, f. 277, Ann. Reps. Matobo 1916 and 1922.
37. In 1916 the district had 8 575 Africans on alienated land and 31 162 in Reserves. The figures in 1922 were 4 200 and 38 415. N/9/1/19, f. 189, N/9/1/25, f. 258, Ann. Reps. Bulalima-Mangwe 1916 and 1922.
38. e.g. N/9/1/24, f. 188, Ann. Rep. Supt. N. Bulawayo 1921.
39. N/3/11/7, f. 121, Bagshawe to C.N.C., 12 May 1922.
40. N/9/4/42, f. 410, Mon. Rep. Melsetter, May 1922.
41. N/9/4/43, f. 1, Mon. Rep. C.N.C., July 1922.
42. N/3/11/7, f. 248, Taylor to Supt. N. Victoria, 11 Mar. 1922.
43. N/9/1/25, f. 106, Ann. Rep. Supt. N. Victoria 1922.
44. Ibid., f. 155a, Ann. Rep. Ndanga 1922.
45. Ibid., f. 168, Ann. Rep. Bikita 1922; South. Rhod., *Rep. C.N.C. 1922,* 2.
46. N/9/4/43, f. 1, Mon. Rep. C.N.C., July 1922.
47. Ibid., f. 280, Mon. Rep. Chilimanzi, September 1922.
48. Ibid., ff. 522, 635, Mon. Reps. Sipolilo, November and December 1922.
49. N. H. W., 'Note on Darwin ritual murder', *NADA* (1926), IV, 61–2; *Zambesi Miss. Rec.* (1922-5), VII (July 1923), 253–6; Bourdillon, *The Shona Peoples,* 253.
50. A/3/18/23, f. 4, Taylor to Adm., 2 May 1923; above, 64.
51. G. J. Van Apeldoorn, *Perspectives on Drought and Famine in Nigeria* (London, Allen & Unwin, 1981), 36; Srivastava, *Indian Famines,* 329.
52. A/3/18/23, ff. 33, 4, Taylor to Adm., 8 Jan. and 2 May 1923.
53. S235/506, Ann. Rep. Inyanga 1928.
54. *Rhod. Her.,* 9 Dec. 1922.
55. N/9/1/25, f. 43, Ann. Rep. Sipolilo 1922.
56. South. Rhod., *Rep. C.N.C.1922,* 6.
57. N/9/4/43, f. 12, Mon. Rep. Buhera, July 1922; N/9/4/44, Mon. Rep. Buhera, February and March 1923. For memories of the suffering in Buhera, see J. F. Holleman, *African Interlude* (Cape Town, Nasionale Boekhandel, 1958), 145–6 (I owe this reference to Dr Beach).
58. N/9/4/43, f. 635, Mon. Rep. Sipolilo, December 1922; N/9/4/44, Mon. Rep. Sipolilo, January 1923.
59. N/9/4/43, f. 25, Mon. Rep. Urungwe, July 1922; N/9/4/44, Mon. Reps. Lomagundi, January 1923, and Urungwe, March 1923.
60. N/9/4/43, f. 164, Mon. Rep. Ndanga, August 1922.

126

61. *Zambesi Miss. Rec.* (1922-5), VII (Oct. 1922), 119.
62. *Rhod. Her.,* 8 Dec. 1922.
63. C. F. Andrews, *John White of Mashonaland* (reprinted, New York, Negro University Press, 1969), 187.
64. Ibid., G. Siqalaba, 183–4.
65. Ibid., A. Shamu, 186.
66. *Zambesi Miss. Rec.* (1922-5), VII (July 1922), 86.
67. Quoted in Mashingaidze, 'Christian Missions', 345.
68. N/3/11/8, f. 75, Edwards to Supt. N. Salisbury, 9 Nov. 1922.
69. N/9/4/42, f. 390, Mon. Rep. Victoria, May 1922.
70. H. De Laessoe, 'The Lundi and Sabi Rivers', *Proceedings of the Rhod. Scientific Association* (1906), VI, 125; N/3/11/8, f. 23, Adm. on C.N.C. to Adm., 13 Jan. 1923.

CHAPTER 8

1. Native Commissioners' monthly and annual reports for 1933 are in S235/526 and S235/511, respectively.
2. See Palmer, *Land and Racial Domination,* 241–2; Mosley, *Settler Economies,* 71–2; Ranger, *Peasant Consciousness,* 54–9.
3. Rhod., *Census 1969,* 5.
4. For the scarcity of 1928, see South. Rhod., *Rep. C.N.C., 1928* (Sess. Pap. C.S.R. 14), 3–4.
5. *Bulawayo Chron.,* 2 Dec. 1933.
6. Mosley, *Settler Economies,* 120.
7. S.O.A.S., Counc. World Miss., South Africa Reports 8/2, J. Whiteside, 'London Missionary Society Annual Report from Tjimali-Dombodema Station, Dec. 31 1933', quoting Rev. Mofiwa Tjuma.
8. J. R. H. Shaul, 'Maize forecasts in Mazoe district of Southern Rhodesia, 1920–42', *South African Journal of Economics* (1943), XI, 294.
9. S235/511, f. 44, Ann. Rep. Mazoe 1933.
10. S235/511, f. 91, Ann. Rep. Lomagundi 1933.
11. N/9/1/25, f. 52 and S235/511, f. 65, Ann. Reps. Marandellas 1922 and 1933.
12. S235/511, f. 298, Ann. Rep. Umtali 1933; S235/526, Mon. Rep. Mtoko, September 1933; S235/511, f. 151, Ann. Rep. Mount Darwin 1933.
13 Sister Mary Aquina, O. P., 'The social background of agriculture in Chilimanzi Reserve', *The Rhodes-Livingstone Journal* (Dec. 1964), XXXVI, 9–10; N/9/1/25, f. 139 and S235/511, f. 245, Ann. Reps. Chilimanzi 1922 and 1933.
14. S235/511, f. 225, Ann. Rep. Chibi 1933.
15. S235/526, Mon. Rep. C.N.C., December 1933; S235/511, f. 339, Ann. Rep. Melsetter 1933.
16. S.O.A.S., Counc. World Miss., South Africa Reports 8/2, Jones, circular letter, 3 Mar. 1933.
17. S235/526, Mon. Rep. C.N.C., March 1933.
18. N/9/1/25, f. 277 and S235/511, f. 442, Ann. Reps. Matobo 1922 and 1933.
19. S235/511, f. 442, Ann. Rep. Matobo 1933.
20. Ibid., f. 356, Ann. Rep. Bulawayo 1933.
21. *Bulawayo Chron.,* 9 Dec. 1933.
22. Mosley, *Settler Economies,* 72; Phimister, 'Meat and monopolies', 410–11.
23. Mosley, *Settler Economies,* 104; S235/511, ff. 517, 524, Ann. Reps. Que Que and Belingwe 1933.
24. S235/526, Mon. Rep. Ndanga, June 1933.
25. South. Rhod., *Rep. C.N.C. 1933,* 3.
26. S235/511, ff. 267, 285, Ann. Reps. Ndanga and Bikita 1933; Mosley, *Settler Economies,* 159.
27. S235/511, f. 490, Ann. Rep. Wankie 1933.
28. Ibid., f. 573, Ann. Rep. Sebungwe 1933.

29. C. F. Keyter, *Maize Control in Southern Rhodesia 1931–1941* (Salisbury, Central Africa Historical Assoc., Local Series 34, 1978), 25.
30. Ibid., 3.
31. Ibid., 1–8; V. E. M. Machingaidze, 'The Development of Settler Capitalist Agriculture in Southern Rhodesia with Particular Reference to the Role of the State, 1908–1939' (London, Univ. of London, Ph.D. thesis, 1980), 495.
32. Keyter, *Maize Control*, 4–5.
33. S235/526, Mon. Reps. Salisbury and Mazoe, June 1933; S235/511, f. 91, Ann. Rep. Lomagundi 1933.
34. *Bulawayo Chron.*, 1933, *passim*.
35. e.g. S235/511, f. 267, Ann. Rep. Ndanga 1933.
36. *Bulawayo Chron.*, 2 Dec. 1933; Keyter, *Maize Control*, 25; Mosley, *Settler Economies*, 92.
37. M. Yudelman, *Africans on the Land* (Cambridge MA, Harvard Univ. Press, 1964), 115.
38. S235/511, f. 267, Ann. Rep. Ndanga 1933.
39. Ibid., f. 30, Ann. Rep. Mrewa 1933. See also Iliffe, *The African Poor*, 155.
40. South. Rhod., *Rep. C.N.C.1933*, 3.
41. See A. S. Cripps, *How Roads Were Made in the Native Reserves of Charter District, Mashonaland, 1934–5* (n. p. , n. d.), 1–2.
42. *Bulawayo Chron.*, 18 Nov. 1933; A. H. Croxton, *Railways of Rhodesia* (Newton Abbot, David and Charles, 1973), 158; Machingaidze, 'The Development of Settler Capitalist Agriculture', 68.
43. South. Rhod., *Rep. C.N.C. 1932* (Sess. Pap. C.S.R.9,1934), 6; S235/506, Ann. Rep. Mazoe 1928.
44. S235/526, Mon. Rep. Melsetter, June 1933.
45. Ibid., Mon. Rep. C.N.C., March 1933.
46. Ibid., Mon. Reps. Inyanga and C.N.C., January 1933, and Umtali, October 1933.

CHAPTER 9

1. Native Commissioners' monthly reports for 1942 are in S1619. Annual reports could not be traced.
2. Greenough, *Prosperity and Misery in Bengal*, viii, 106–40; Iliffe, *The African Poor*, 157–9.
3. *Bulawayo Chron.*, 13 Feb. 1942.
4. S1619, Mon. Rep. C.N.C., December 1941.
5. Scudder, *The Ecology of the Gwembe Tonga*, 219.
6. Rep. C.N.C., 1943, in South. Rhod., *Reps. Secr. N. Affs. and C.N.C., 1941, 1942, 1943, 1944 and 1945*, 112.
7. S1619, Mon. Rep. Hartley, December 1942.
8. Ibid., Mon. Rep. Gwanda, February 1942.
9. Ibid., Mon. Rep. Matobo, February 1942.
10. Ibid., Mon. Rep. Matobo, October 1942.
11. Ibid., Mon. Rep. Gwanda, December 1942.
12. Ibid., Mon. Reps. Matobo, Gwelo, Bulawayo, and Bubi, December 1942.
13. Rep. C.N.C., 1943, in South. Rhod., *Reps. Secr. N. Affs. and C.N.C., 1941, 1942, 1943, 1944 and 1945*, 113.
14. S1619, Mon. Reps. Gwanda, February and November 1942.
15. Rep. Secr. N. Affs., C.N.C., 1941, in South. Rhod., *Reps. Secr. N. Affs. and C.N.C., 1941, 1942, 1943, 1944 and 1945*, 6; id. *1938*, 1.
16. See Zachrisson, *An African Area in Change: Belingwe*, 201.
17. Mosley, *Settler Economies*, 150.
18. Ibid., 159–60.

19. Rep. Secr. N. Affs., C.N.C., 1942, in South. Rhod., *Reps. Secr. N. Affs. and C.N.C., 1941, 1942, 1943, 1944 and 1945*, 61–2.
20. See Keyter, *Maize Control*, 10–23.
21. Ibid., 28.
22. South. Rhod., *Rep. Secr. N. Affs. and C.N.C., 1940* (Sess.Pap. C.S.R.13, 1941), 4.
23. South. Rhod., *Rep. C.N.C. 1933* (Sess. Pap. C.S.R.9, 1934), 1; Rep. Secr. N. Affs., C.N.C., 1941, in South. Rhod., *Reps. Secr. N. Affs. and C.N.C., 1941, 1942, 1943, 1944 and 1945*, 3; Rhod., *Census 1969*, 5.
24. Yudelman, *Africans on the Land*, 237–8.
25. Zachrisson, *An African Area in Change: Belingwe*, 191.
26. Mosley, *Settler Economies*, 72.
27. Ibid., 121.
28. Ibid., 92.
29. *Bulawayo Chron.*, 13 Feb. and 11 Dec. 1942; South. Rhod., *Debates of the Legislative Assembly*, XXI, cc. 3, 113, 11 Feb. 1942; Mosley, *Settler Economies*, 92.
30. *Bulawayo Chron.*, 30 Jan., 13 Feb. and 6 Mar. 1942.
31. S1619, Mon. Rep. Bulawayo, February 1942.
32. *Bulawayo Chron.*, 1942, *passim*.
33. S1619, Mon. Rep. Hartley, December 1942.
34. S1044/5, Carbutt, circular no. 58, 'Famine relief', n. d. [received Fort Victoria 10 May 1941].
35. S1619, Mon. Rep. Hartley, December 1942.
36. Ibid., Mon. Reps. Gwelo, Salisbury, Matopo, Bubi, Bulawayo, Concession and Chipinga, December 1942.

CHAPTER 10

1. Native Commissioners' annual reports for 1947 are in S1051; a few monthly reports are in S1619.
2. *Bulawayo Chron.*, 10 Jan. 1947.
3. Mosley, *Settler Economies*, 92; South. Rhod., *Rep. Secr. N. Affs., C.N.C., 1947* (Sess. Pap. C.S.R.20, 1948), 13.
4. These figures are from Rep. Secr. N. Affs., C.N.C. 1943, in South. Rhod., *Reps. Secr. N. Affs. and C.N.C., 1941, 1942, 1943, 1944 and 1945*, 117.
5. R. W. M. Johnson, 'African agricultural development in Southern Rhodesia, 1945–1960', *Food Research Institute Studies* (1964), IV, 216.
6. Rhod., *Census 1969*, 5–6.
7. Roder, 'The division of land resources', 51.
8. Rep. Secr. N. Affs., C.N.C., 1941, in South. Rhod., *Reps. Secr. N. Affs. and C.N.C., 1941, 1942, 1943, 1944 and 1945*, 3; id. *1948* (Sess. Pap. C.S.R.27, 1949), 6.
9. Machingaidze, 'The Development of Settler Capitalist Agriculture', 255, 279.
10. R. Riddell, *The Land Question* (Gwelo, Mambo Press, 1978), 11.
11. L. H. Gann and P. Duignan, *White Settlers in Tropical Africa* (Harmondsworth, Penguin, 1962), 159–60.
12. Ranger, *Peasant Consciousness*, 170; S235/511, f. 331, Ann. Rep. Makoni 1933; S1051, Ann. Rep. Rusape 1947.
13. South. Rhod., *Rep. Secr. N. Affs., C.N.C. 1946* (Sess. Pap. C.S.R.48, 1947), 5.
14. Id. *1947*, 34.
15. See S1044/5, A. G. Yardley, 'Drought conditions and stock: Victoria district', 12 Feb. 1947.
16. South. Rhod., *Rep. Secr. N. Affs., C.N.C., 1947*, 19.
17. Id. *1946*, 2; above, 107.
18. South. Rhod., *Rep. Secr. N. Affs., C.N.C., 1949* (Sess. Pap. C.S.R.27, 1950), 71; Mosley, *Settler Economies*, 72.

19. S1051, Ann. Rep. Mazoe 1947.
20. S235/511, f. 245 and S1051, Ann. Reps. Chilimanzi 1933 and 1947.
21. S235/511, f. 256 and S1051, Ann. Reps. Gutu 1933 and 1947; South. Rhod., *Rep. Secr. N. Affs.*, *C.N.C., 1947*, 19.
22. S1044/5, N.C. Gutu to P.N.C. Victoria, 10 Feb. 1947.
23. Ibid., N.C. Nuanetsi to P.N.C. Victoria, 15 Jan. and 11 Feb. 1947. For the suffering in the south, see Holleman, *African Interlude*, 145.
24. South. Rhod., *Rep. Secr. N. Affs.*, *C.N.C. 1946*, 42.
25. S1051, Ann. Rep. Darwin 1947.
26. Ibid., Ann. Rep. Urungwe 1947.
27. Ibid., Ann. Rep. Sebungwe 1947.
28. Ibid., Ann. Rep. Gwanda 1947.
29. S1619, Mon. Rep. Lupani, January 1947.
30. S1044/5, C.N.C., '1947 drought', *c.*14 Feb. 1947.
31. *Bulawayo Chron.*, 4 Apr., 2 May and 12 Sept. 1947.
32. South. Rhod., *Rep. Secr. N. Affs.*, *C.N.C., 1947*, 13; S1044/5, N.C. Gutu to P.N.C. Victoria, 5 Jan. 1948.
33. South. Rhod., *Rep. Secr. N. Affs.*, *C.N.C., 1947*, 3; S1044/5, N.C. Gutu to P.N.C. Victoria, 5 Jan. 1948; *35284, Q. Rep. Gutu, July-September 1948.
34. South. Rhod., *Rep. Secr. N. Affs.*, *C.N.C., 1947*, 16, 5.
35. S1051, Ann. Rep. Belingwe 1947. See also Kosmin, '"Freedom, Justice and Commerce"', 31.
36. Mosley, *Settler Economies*, 92; South. Rhod., *Debates of the Legislative Assembly*, XXVI, cc. 2, 874, 26 Feb. 1947; S1051, Ann. Reps. Mtoko and Sinoia 1947.
37. S1051, Ann. Rep. Gwanda 1947.
38. Ibid., Ann. Rep. Sebungwe 1947.
39. Ibid., Ann. Rep. Chibi 1947.
40. *Bulawayo Chron.*, 12 Sept. 1947.
41. South. Rhod., *Rep. Secr. N. Affs.*, *C.N.C., 1947*, 2.
42. Mosley, *Settler Economies*, 108; South. Rhod., *Rep. Secr. N. Affs.*, *C.N.C., 1947*, 22, 15.
43. Mosley, *Settler Economies*, 150.
44. *Bulawayo Chron.*, 21 Mar. 1947.
45. Ibid., 26 Sept. 1947.
46. Mosley, *Settler Economies*, 160; S1051, Ann. Reps. Rusape, Marandellas and Sinoia, 1947.
47. S1051, Ann. Rep. Chilimanzi 1947.
48. Ibid., Ann. Rep. Nyamandhlovu 1947.
49. Ibid., Ann. Rep. Bubi 1947.
50. Ibid., Ann. Rep. Bikita 1947; South. Rhod., *Rep. Public Health, 1949* (Sess. Pap. C.S.R.25, 1950), 9; *35284, Q. Rep. C.N.C., July-September 1948.
51. S1051, Ann. Reps. Chibi and Sebungwe 1947.
52. See South. Rhod. and Federation of Rhod. and Nyasaland, Ministry of Health, Ann. Reps. Nutrition Counc. (South. Rhod.), 1948–58.
53. South. Rhod., *Rep. Public Health, 1949*, 44.

CHAPTER 11

1. *71881 contains Native Commissioners' annual reports for 1960. (I am grateful to Mr B. Duehohn for drawing my attention to this file.) Monthly reports have not been found.
2. Mosley, *Settler Economies*, 72.
3. Johnson, 'Agricultural development', 179.
4. Mosley, *Settler Economies*, 92–3.
5. R. B. Sutcliffe, 'Stagnation and inequality in Rhodesia 1946–1968', *Bulletin of the Oxford University Institute of Economics and Statistics* (1971), XXXIII, 36.

6. S1051 and *71881/11, Ann. Reps. Mazoe 1947 and 1960.
7. P. Hamilton, 'Population pressure and land use in Chiweshe Reserve', *Rhodes-Livingstone Journal* (Dec. 1964), XXXVI, 42, 51–2.
8. R. W. M. Johnson, 'An economic survey of Chiweshe Reserve', ibid., 93.
9. Hamilton, 'Population pressure', 53.
10. S1051, Ann. Rep. Rusape 1947; *71881/39, Ann. Rep. Makoni 1960.
11. *71881/12, Ann. Rep. Mount Darwin 1960.
12. S1051 and *71881/20, Ann. Reps. Gutu 1947 and 1960.
13. *71881/11, Ann. Rep. Chipinga 1960; Roder, *The Sabi Valley Irrigation Projects*, 13.
14. *71881/9, Ann. Rep. Chibi 1960.
15. *71881/35, Ann. Rep. Nuanetsi 1960.
16. *71881/5, Ann. Rep. Binga 1960.
17. Weinrich, *The Tonga People*, 19.
18. *71881/36, Ann. Rep. Nyamandhlovu 1960.
19. South. Rhod., *Rep. Secr. N. Affs., C.N.C. 1960* (Sess. Pap. C.S.R.28, 1961), 89–90.
20. *71881/42, 21, 1, Ann. Reps. Shabani, Gwanda, and Beit Bridge, 1960.
21. Rhod., *Census 1969*, 5.
22. Palmer, *Land and Racial Domination*, 185; South. Rhod., *Rep. Secr. N. Affs., C.N.C., 1948*, 6; id. *1961* (Sess. Pap. C.S.R.28, 1962), 5; Roder, 'The division of land resources', 48; W. J. Barber, *The Economy of British Central Africa* (London, Oxford Univ. Press, 1961), 137; *Bulawayo Chron.*, 17 August 1960.
23. *Bulawayo Chron.*, 8 Jan. and 9 Nov. 1960; Mosley, *Settler Economies*, 92–3.
24. Mosley, *Settler Economies*, 120.
25. Ibid., 160, 150–1.
26. Sutcliffe, 'Stagnation and inequality in Rhodesia', 35.
27. D. G. Clarke, *Unemployment and Economic Structure in Rhodesia* (Gwelo, Mambo Press, 1977), 8–9.
28. *71881/36, Ann. Rep. Nyamandhlovu 1960; *Bulawayo Chron.*, 18 Apr. 1960.
29. Mosley, *Settler Economies*, 72.
30. South. Rhod., *Rep. Secr. N. Affs., C.N.C. 1958* (Sess. Pap. C.S.R.25, 1959), 105; id. *1959* (Sess. Pap. C.S.R.18, 1960), 125; id. *1960*, 102.
31. Id. *1960*, 108; *71881/16 and 34, Ann. Reps. Victoria and Nkai 1960.
32. Above, 106.
33. Mosley, *Settler Economies*, 72.
34. A. K. H. Weinrich, *African Farmers in Rhodesia* (London, Oxford Univ. Press, 1975), 83; M. Bratton, *Beyond Community Development: The Political Economy of Rural Administration in Zimbabwe* (Gwelo, Mambo Press, 1978), 9.
35. Yudelman, *Africans on the Land*, 121–6; Ranger, *Peasant Consciousness*, 75; W. Allan, *The African Husbandman* (Edinburgh, Oliver and Boyd, 1967), 426; Weinrich, *African Farmers in Rhodesia*, 60.
36. *71881/20, Ann. Rep. Gutu 1960.
37. B. F. Massell, and R. W. M. Johnson, *African Agriculture in Rhodesia: An Econometric Survey* (Santa Monica, Rand Corp., 1966), 49. See also Aquina, 'The social background of agriculture', 34.
38. *71881/35, Ann. Rep. Nuanetsi 1960.
39. *71881/4, Ann. Rep. Bindura 1960.
40. South. Rhod., *Rep. Secr. N. Affs., C.N.C. 1960*, 42.
41. *Bulawayo Chron.*, 3 Feb. 1960.
42. South. Rhod., *Rep. Secr. N. Affs., C.N.C. 1960*, 93.
43. *71881/16 and 9, Ann. Reps. Victoria and Chibi 1960.
44. *71881/2, 16, 42, Ann. Reps. Belingwe, Victoria, and Shabani, 1960.
45. *71881/37, Ann. Rep. Bulalima Mangwe 1960.

46. *71881/16, Ann. Rep. Victoria 1960.
47. *71881/38, Ann. Rep. Que Que 1960.
48. *71881/27, Ann. Rep. Lupane 1960; Federation of Rhod. and Nyasaland, *Rep. Public Health, 1960* (Sess. Paps. 184, 1961), 8–9.
49. N. F. Lyons and B. P. B. Ellis, 'Leprosy in Zimbabwe', *Leprosy Review* (1983), LIV, 46.
50. *71881/42 and 46, Ann. Reps. Shabani and Gwaai Reserve 1960.
51. Federation of Rhod. and Nyasaland, *Rep. Public Health, 1960*, 22.
52. *71881, Ann. Reps.
53. Federation of Rhod. and Nyasaland, Ministry of Health, 'Ann. Rep. Nutrition Counc. (South. Rhod.) for 1954'.
54. Gelfand, *Diet and Tradition*, 194–6, 215, 219–20.
55. Federation of Rhod. and Nyasaland, Ministry of Health, 'Ann. Rep., 1958: Food Technologist', enclosed in 'Ann. Rep. Nutrition Counc. (South. Rhod.) for 1957 and 1958'.
56. Federation of Rhod. and Nyasaland, Ministry of Health, 'Ann. Rep. Nutrition Counc. (South. Rhod.) for 1957 and 1958'.
57. World Bank, *Population Growth and Policies in Sub-Saharan Africa* (Washington DC, The Bank, 1986), 37.
58. Riddell, *The Land Question*, 9; Watts, *Silent Violence*, 7.
59. Rhod., *Rep. Secr. Internal Affs. 1964* (Sess. Pap. C.S.R.39, 1965), 12; id. *1965* (Sess. Pap. C.S.R.34, 1966), 6–8; id. *1970* (Sess. Pap. Cmd R.R. 30, 1971), 1–2; Bourdillon, *The Shona Peoples*, xi; R. Leys, 'Drought and drought relief in southern Zimbabwe', in P. Lawrence (ed.), *World Recession and the Food Crisis in Africa* (London, James Currey, 1986), ch. 20; M. Bratton, 'Drought, food and the social organization of small farmers in Zimbabwe', in Glantz, *Drought and Hunger*, ch. 10; *Herald*, 8 and 28 July 1986; *Moto* (Gweru) (1987), LIV, 11.
60. Bratton, 'Drought, food and the social organization of small farmers', 237.
61. Leys, 'Drought and drought relief in southern Zimbabwe', 263–4.

CHAPTER 12

1. Watts, *Silent Violence*, 464.

# Select Bibliography

Abraham, D. P. 'The early political history of the Kingdom of Mwene Mutapa (850–1589)', in *Historians in Tropical Africa: Proceedings of the Leverhulme Inter-Collegiate History Conference, Held at the University College of Rhodesia and Nyasaland, September 1960* (Salisbury, Univ. College of Rhodesia and Nyasaland, 1962), 61–91.

Andrews, C. F. *John White of Mashonaland* (London, Hodder & Stoughton, 1935 [reprint: New York, Negro Univ. Press, 1969])

Aquina, Sister Mary, O.P. See Weinrich, A. K. H.

Baden-Powell, R. S. S. *The Matabele Campaign 1896* (London, Methuen, 1896 [1897] [4th edn, 1901]).

Beach, D. N. 'Second thoughts on the Shona economy: Suggestions for further research', *Rhodesian History* (1976), VII, 1–11.

*Zimbabwe before 1900* (Gweru, Mambo Press, 1984).

'Zimbabwean Demography: Early Colonial Data' (Milwaukee, Conference on the Analysis of Census Data from Colonial Central Africa, 1986).

Bhila, H. H. K. *Trade and Politics in a Shona Kingdom: The Manyika and Their African and Portuguese Neighbours 1575–1902* (Harlow, Longman, 1982).

Bourdillon, M. F. C. *The Shona Peoples* (Gweru, Mambo Press, 2nd edn, 1982).

British South Africa Company. *Report on the Company's Proceedings and the Condition of the Territories within the Sphere of Its Operations, 1896–1897* ( [London, The Company, 1898]).

Burke, E. E. (ed.). *The Journals of Carl Mauch*, trans. F. O. Bernhard (Salisbury, National Archives of Rhodesia, 1969).

Carnegie, D. *Among the Matabele* (London, The Religious Tract Society, 2nd edn, 1894).

Chidziwa, J. 'History of the Vashawasha', *NADA* (1964), IX, i, 16–33.

Cobbing, J. R. D. 'The Ndebele under the Khumalos, 1820–1896' (Lancaster, Univ. of Lancaster, Ph.D. thesis, 1976).

Collins, M. O. (ed.). *Rhodesia: Its Natural Resources and Economic Development* (Salisbury, M. O. Collins, 1965).

Cripps, A. S. *Lyra Evangelistica: Missionary Verses of Mashonaland* (Oxford, B. H. Blackwell, 1909).

Edwards, W. 'The Wanoe: A short historical sketch', *NADA* (1926), IV, 13–28.

Fyfe, C. and McMaster, D. (eds.). *African Historical Demography: Volume II* (Edinburgh, Univ. of Edinburgh, Centre of African Studies, 1981).

Fynes-Clinton, S. H. (ed.). 'Mavunga Madziwadzira: Headman Madzima recalls', *NADA* (1970), X, ii, 31–5.

Gelfand, M. *Diet and Tradition in an African Culture* (Edinburgh, Livingstone, 1971).

Glantz, M. H. (ed.) *Drought and Hunger in Africa: Denying Famine a Future* (Cambridge, Cambridge Univ. Press, 1987).

Great Britain. *Report by Sir R. E. R. Martin, K. C. M. G., on the Native Administration of the British South Africa Company* . . . [C. 8547], 561–688 (H.C. 1897, lxii).

Great Britain, Colonial Office. Africa (South) 717: 'Further Correspondence [1903] Relative to Affairs in the Bechuanaland Protectorate and Rhodesia' (in Public Record Office, Confidential Print, Africa [C.O. 879/79]).

Greenough, P. R. *Prosperity and Misery in Modern Bengal: The Famine of 1943–1944* (New York, Oxford Univ. Press, 1982).

Hamilton, P. 'Population pressure and land use in Chiweshe Reserve', *Rhodes-Livingstone Journal* (Dec. 1964), XXXVI, 40–58.

Holleman, J. F. *African Interlude* (Cape Town, Nasionale Boekhandel, 1958).

Iliffe, J. *The African Poor: A History* (Cambridge, Cambridge Univ. Press, 1987).

Johnson, R. W. M. 'African agricultural development in Southern Rhodesia, 1945–1960', *Food Research Institute Studies* (1964), IV, ii, 165–223.

Keyter, C. F. *Maize Control in Southern Rhodesia 1931–1941: The African Contribution to White Survival* (Salisbury, The Central Africa Historical Association, Local Series 34, 1978).

Klein, I. 'When the rains failed: Famine, relief, and mortality in British India', *Indian Economic and Social History Review* (1984), XXI, 185–214.

Kosmin, B. A. '"Freedom, Justice and Commerce": Some factors affecting Asian trading patterns in Southern Rhodesia, 1897–1942', *Rhodesian History* (1975), VI, 15–32.

Lawrence, P. (ed.) *World Recession and the Food Crisis in Africa* (London, James Currey, 1986).

Machingaidze, V. E. M. 'The Development of Settler Capitalist Agriculture in Southern Rhodesia with Particular Reference to the Role of the State, 1908–1939' (London, Univ. of London, Ph.D. thesis, 1980).

Mashingaidze, E. K. 'Christian Missions in Mashonaland, Southern Rhodesia, 1890–1930' (York, Univ. of York, Ph.D. thesis, 1973).

McAlpin, M. B. *Subject to Famine: Food Crises and Economic Change in Western India, 1860–1920* (Princeton, Princeton Univ. Press, 1983).

Miller, J. C. 'The significance of drought, disease and famine in the agriculturally marginal zones of West-Central Africa', *Journal of African History* (1982), XXIII, 17–61.

Mosley, P. *The Settler Economies: Studies in the Economic History of Kenya and Southern Rhodesia 1900–1963* (Cambridge, Cambridge Univ. Press, 1983).

Olivier, S. P. *Many Treks Made Rhodesia* [transl.1943] (Cape Town, Timmins, 1957 [ reprint: Bulawayo, Books of Rhodesia, 1975]).

Palmer, R. H. *Land and Racial Domination in Rhodesia* (London, Heinemann, 1977).

Palmer, R. H. and Parsons, Q. N. (eds.). *The Roots of Rural Poverty in Central and Southern Africa* (London, Heinemann, 1977).

Posselt, F. W. T. *Fact and Fiction: A Short Account of the Natives of Southern Rhodesia* (Bulawayo, Rhodesian Printing & Publishing, 1935 [reprint: Bulawayo, Books of Rhodesia, 1978]).

Ranger, T. O. *Peasant Consciousness and Guerrilla War in Zimbabwe* (London, James Currey, 1985).

Rhodesia. *Census of Population 1969* (Salisbury [1971?]).

Riddell, R. *The Land Question* (Gwelo, Mambo Press, 1978).

Roder, W. 'The division of land resources in Southern Rhodesia', *Annals of the Association of American Geographers* (1964), LIV, 41–58.

Roder, W. *The Sabi Valley Irrigation Projects* (Chicago, Univ. of Chicago, Dep. of

135

Geography, 1965).

Scudder, T. *The Ecology of the Gwembe Tonga* (Manchester, Manchester Univ. Press, 1962).

Selous, F. C. *Sunshine and Storm in Rhodesia* (London, Rowland Ward, 1896 [reprint: Bulawayo, Books of Rhodesia, 1968]).

Sen, A. *Poverty and Famines* (Oxford, Clarendon, revised edn, 1982).

Southern Rhodesia. *Returns of a Census Taken on 17th April, 1904* (Sessional Paper, A.23, 1904).

Srivastava, H. S. *The History of Indian Famines and Development of Famine Policy (1858–1918)* (Agra, Mehra, 1968).

Sutcliffe, R. B. 'Stagnation and inequality in Rhodesia 1946–1968', *Bulletin of the Oxford Institute of Economics and Statistics* (1971), XXXIII, 35–56.

Taylor, J. J. 'The Emergence and Development of the Native Department in Southern Rhodesia, 1894–1914' (London, Univ. of London, Ph.D. thesis, 1974).

Thomas, T. M. *Eleven Years in Central South Africa.* (London, J. Snow, 1872 [2nd edn, 1971]).

Vaughan, M. *The Story of an African Famine: Gender and Famine in Twentieth-century Malawi* (Cambridge, Cambridge Univ. Press, 1987).

Watts, M. *Silent Violence: Food, Famine and Peasantry in Northern Nigeria* (Berkeley, Univ. of California Press, 1983).

Weinrich, A. K. H. 'The social background of agriculture in Chilimanzi Reserve', *Rhodes-Livingstone Journal* (Dec. 1964), XXXVI, 7–39.

      *African Farmers in Rhodesia: Old and New Peasant Communities in Karangaland* (London, Oxford Univ. Press for Int. African Inst., 1975).

      *The Tonga People on the Southern Shore of Lake Kariba* (Gwelo, Mambo Press, 1977).

Yudelman, M. *Africans on the Land* (Cambridge MA, Harvard Univ. Press, 1964).

Zachrisson, P. *An African Area in Change: Belingwe 1894–1946* (Gothenburg, Univ. of Gothenburg, 1978).

# INDEX

Abraham, D.P., 16-17
Afrikaners, 22-3, 32-3, 72
agricultural systems, 14-15, 32-3, 43, 57-8, 78, 80, 86, 92-3, 97-9, 103-4

Bazeley, W.S., 43-52, 55, 65-7, 69
Beach, D.N., 8
Belingwe District, 25, 32, 39, 53, 60, 63, 69-70, 74-5, 83-4, 99-100, 108
Bhila, H.H.K., 17
Bikita District, 47, 49-50, 52, 56, 64-7, 72, 74-5, 82, 86, 98, 102
Bindura District, 108
Blackwell, C.S., 47, 52
British South Africa Company, 21-2, 24-7, 31, 38, 41, 55
British South Africa Police, 49, 51
Bubi District, 22, 54, 62, 69, 92, 94
Buhera sub-district, 60, 62, 76
Bulalima-Mangwe District, 25, 32, 53-4, 60, 62, 71-3, 108
Bulawayo, 23, 25-7, 31, 33, 37, 45, 54, 56-7, 62, 64, 68-70, 81, 83, 89, 91, 93-4, 96, 103, 106, 113
Bushu Reserve, 104

capitalism, 8-9, 11, 68, 80-1, 88-9, 96, 103, 106-8, 110-11
Carbutt, C.L., 47, 78, 87, 94
cattle, 15, 18, 21, 28, 32, 43-4, 46-7, 51, 54, 60-1, 65, 69-70, 72, 75, 82-4, 91, 93, 98-9, 101, 104, 106-7
Chaminuka, 20
Chaplin, F.P.D., 62-4
Charter Disrict, 32-3, 37, 59, 61-2, 73-4
Chibi District, 18, 34, 42-4, 46-7, 49-50, 52-3, 55, 60, 82, 98, 101, 105, 108, 110
Chikwizo Reserve, 82
Chilimanzi District, 57, 60, 74, 82, 98, 109
China, 9
Chipinga District, 94, 109

Chishawasha Mission, 32-3
Chiweshe Reserve, 72, 104, 107
Chizwiti, Chief, 75
Concession District, 94
Cripps, A.S., 33, 36, 41

Dandawa, Chief, 34, 38
Dande, see Mount Darwin District
disease, 16-20, 26, 28, 35-7, 52-3, 58, 64, 69, 83, 88, 94-5, 102, 109
Dutt, R.C., 8
Dzivaguru, 16

Edwards, W., 70
Embakwe Mission, 53
Empandeni Mission, 22, 29, 53-5, 57, 72, 76
European settlement, 10-11, 22-3, 31, 43-4, 56, 61-2, 72-3, 79, 82, 93, 96-8, 105-6

Filabusi District, 22, 54, 109
Forrestall, P., 47, 52-3
Fort Victoria District, 32, 43, 45-7, 51-2, 56-7, 65, 68, 74, 78, 81, 89-90, 96, 98, 103, 105, 107-9, 113
Fynn, H.C.K., 35-6, 41

Gelfand, M., 109
Gielgud, V., 28
Goromonzi District, 109
Grain Marketing Board, 106-7, 110
Grey, Earl, 21, 25, 29
Grey, Lady, 26
Gutu District, 18, 20, 33, 37, 46, 59-60, 69-70, 74, 98, 100, 104, 107, 109
Gwaai Reserve, 72, 90-1, 108-9
Gwanda District, 54, 57, 60-1, 68, 70, 83, 89-91, 94, 99, 101, 106-7
Gwelo District, 43, 69-70, 83, 94, 105, 109

Hartley District, 33, 39-40, 61, 90, 94, 98

137

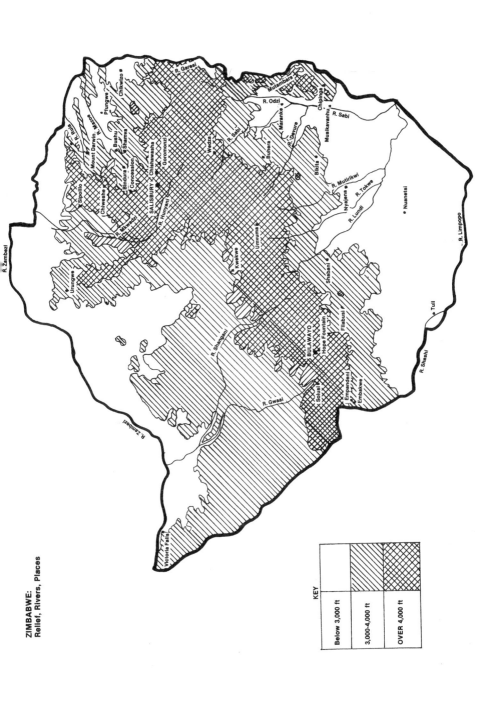

ZIMBABWE:
Relief, Rivers, Places

KEY

Below 3,000 ft

3,000–4,000 ft

OVER 4,000 ft

SOUTHERN RHODESIA:
Administrative Districts, 1916

Mtoko

Inyanga

Melsetter

Mrewa

Makoni

Umtali

Mount Darwin

Ndanga

Mazoe

Salisbury

Marandellas

Charter

Gutu

Chibi

Fort Victoria

Chilimanzi

Lomagundi

Hartley

Selukwe

Belingwe

Gwelo

Insiza

Gwanda

Mzingwane

Sebungwe

Matopo

Bubi

Bulawayo

Bulalima-Mangwe

Nyamandhlovu

Wankie